Reagan vs. Qaddafi:

Response to International Terrorism?

Preface

On April 14, 1986 the United States, having announced its intention to raise the costs of terrorism, launched an attack on Libyan targets in what President Reagan would later say was in retaliation for the direct Libyan role in the West German nightclub bombing...

We know that terrorism has been a menace to American soil for many years; decades before September 11, 2001. Has our government adequately responded to international terrorism in the past? Are we currently? Are the Bush objectives to decapitate Saddam Hussein similar to that of the Reagan Administrations' attempt on Qaddafi?

This book presents information, perspective and commentary on the April 15, 1986 raid on Libya, and circumstances resulting in and around that raid. Read on, and draw your own conclusions.

Introduction

The 1986 raid on Libya was not solely a response to international terrorism, as the Reagan Administration proclaimed, but according to my research, it was a predetermined objective intended to decapitate the leadership of the Libyan regime.

The focus and concentration of this book will be on the April 15, 1986 raid on Libya (a.k.a. Operation El Dorado Canyon), and the reasons behind it. To fully understand the circumstances and reasons that led to the raid, we must look past the issue of terrorism and even past the raid itself.

We must take a closer look at the Reagan Administration and especially examine its conduct and formulation of foreign policy, along with a look at some legal issues pertaining to actions taken by the Reagan Administration.

To begin, one must understand the conservative frame of mind during that Administration. It is much like the current mindset after the September 11, 2001 terrorist attacks.

We are all aware that terrorism was a world concern during the early and mid 1980s, and that the accepted belief was that the raid was only retaliation against terrorism. By questioning past assumptions regarding the Reagan Administration's reason for the raid, new insights can be found.

The reason behind the raid may lie elsewhere, and through close analysis of the Reagan Doctrine and the Administration's foreign policy during the early 1980s, more possibilities will come to light.

Table of Contents

Reagan vs. Qaddafi:

Response to International Terrorism?

R.A. Davidson III

Dedication

This book is dedicated to all those who read it. I sincerely hope that it stimulates theory, thought, imagination, controversy, or is merely found to be enjoyable reading. *This was written for you, so please enjoy!*

Acknowledgements

I would like to acknowledge the outstanding college educators from whom I have had the privilege of gaining knowledge during my many years in the world of academia.

I would like to specifically thank Dr. Girma Negash and Dr. Robert (Bob) Botsch, professors at the University of South Carolina at Aiken, for all the wisdom, knowledge and support provided during my early academic days. Dr. Negash was specifically instrumental in my development of much of this material.

In supporting my thesis that the 1986 raid on Libya was not solely a response to international terrorism, but a predetermined objective, we must look at the culmination of a series of developments in U.S. foreign policy and military strategy.

We will also look briefly at international terrorism, the Reagan Administration's foreign policy and decision-making process, the confrontations between Reagan and Qaddafi, and finally, at the reasons why Reagan would want to decapitate the Libyan regime, or see Qaddafi overthrown.

Chapter 1

Terrorism Defined

On April 14, 1986, the United States, having announced its intention to raise the costs of terrorism, launched an attack on Libyan targets in what President Reagan would later say was in retaliation for the direct Libyan role in the West German nightclub bombing. It had been determined as stated by the Reagan Administration that Libya's leader, Colonel Qaddafi, was supporting anti-U.S. terrorism, including the bombing of a German Discotheque that killed American soldiers in the blast. In addition, the Libyans were claiming the Gulf of Sidra, scene of the famous naval battle in the Second World War, as territorial waters. Three carriers were deployed to the region: the USS America, the USS Saratoga and the USS Coral Sea. This was to underline America's position that this was international water and ships of any nation had the right of free passage. This was to set the stage for the F/A-18 Hornet's baptism of fire.

In all, 100 U.S. aircraft took part in the operation, code-named El Dorado Canyon. Of this number, thirteen Air Force F-111 tactical strike bombers based in England and twelve carrier-based Navy A-6 Intruder attack aircraft simultaneously bombed five specific ground targets in and around the cities of Tripoli and Benghazi, and struck at numerous surface-to-air missile sites dotted across northern Libya.

The U.S. actions against Libya however, started long before 1986 and continued long after that year, as the following demonstrates:

- In 1972, Washington refused to conduct any dialogue or any diplomatic relations at the ambassadorial level with Libya.

- On 30 May 1973, a U.S. aircraft entered Libyan air space during the maneuvers of the Sixth Fleet.

- In 1974 the delivery of 8 DC 1309 planes to Libya was blocked, despite the previous payment of $60,000 in cash.

- On 3 January 1975 the U.S. Secretary of State threatened to use force against oil-producing countries.

- In 1977 the Pentagon put the Jamahiriya on its list of enemies of the USA.

- In 1978 the USA waged an undeclared economic war against the Jamahiriya with the aim of discontinuing Libya's export business, including the delivery of Boeing planes for civilian air traffic.

- In 1981, U.S. navy jets shot down two Libyan Air Force jets over the Mediterranean and a lot more actions against Libya followed.

- On 25 March 1986, the USA violated the UN Charter and international law when Navy planes in the Mediterranean near the Gulf of Sirte bombarded civilian targets in the Gulf along with a Coast Guard boat that was on a routine reconnaissance trip. Furthermore, a Coast Guard ship, which was also on a routine reconnaissance trip in Libyan territorial waters, was attacked. The brutal result of this adventure was the death of the entire crew.

- On April 14, 1986, the United States launched an air attack against targets in Libya. The American official justification for the 1986 air and sea raids on Libya was self-defense, but up to date there has not been any evidence of Libya's involvement in the Berlin bombings, which means the 1986 attacks were planned long before the Berlin incident.

American writer Jim Taylor, in his book, *Man or Myth* wrote:

> History tells us that about 175 years ago, pasha-led pirates ensconced in Tripoli demanded and received tribute from American ships on the shores of that Mediterranean port city. But in today's 'New World Order' it is the United States of America that is using piracy against the small nation of Libya via both vituperative rhetoric and murderous military attacks that would do justice to the Japanese treachery culminating in the 1941 surprise attack upon Pearl Harbor. Was not President Ronald Reagan's vicious raid on Libya in the middle of the night to make an attempt to kill the leader of Libya also a 'surprise attack?' Was it not planned in secret at the White House in exactly the same manner as the Japanese naval command prepared for the Pearl Harbor attack?

There was not even any American ambassador in Tripoli to discuss matters with as the Japanese diplomats did in November of 1941. Why were the Japanese called traitorous at Pearl Harbor while the Americans sent to kill civilians in Tripoli were called patriotic? Does anyone see a difference between the two attacks? Even if Libya had done wrong, two wrongs do not make it right--nor do they make it even. What could possibly have been our overriding interests?

The official justification for the 1986 air and sea raid on Libya, as stated by President Ronald Reagan and echoed by his Cabinet, was self-defense (to prevent any more terrorist attacks on American citizens abroad).

Christopher Ficek wrote, "... this U.S. military intervention remains a unique situation. Never before in American history had the fight against terrorism been the primary justification for committing U.S. troops to direct combat."

Since the 1986 incident, there have been no other interventions of this sort, until recently in Afghanistan. All other actions have been fought under a banner of a different color. Libya, therefore, is an anomaly and an exception to the rule.

During the Cold War, 1949-1991, every U.S. intervention was framed by the polarization of the time, the struggle of the United States versus the Soviet Union. Libya broke this time-tested mold. Even the chaos of the post-Cold War era has not produced this type deviation from the traditional foreign intervention pattern. Until the events of September 11, 2001, the U.S. has not directly used the armed forces to combat terrorism since the Libya incident.

Because of this stark break with the tradition of U.S. foreign policy, one must wonder if the fight against terrorism is really the primary cause of the Libya attack.

According to the Reagan administration, the raid was intended to be punishing, with high-visibility target damage, and to demonstrate to present and future enemies that the United States did not need to have an aircraft carrier nearby for them to fear retaliation. One must wonder however, what the real reasons were for the raid and what impact they have had on the United States since.

It is important at the outset to clarify conceptual questions about some of the definitions, provide a number of critical facts about some incidents, and finally outline U.S. policy on terrorism during the Reagan Administration.

In order to understand the issues surrounding the raid on Libya, we need to understand the complexities surrounding terrorism, where even a definition is not an easy thing to establish.

Scholars have written many books, journals, etc., just trying to define terrorism. This book will certainly not try to settle this definitional dispute. Even the (then) Vice President of the United States, George Bush, Sr., said that terrorism is easier to describe than define and that the United States has not adopted an official definition of terrorism.

Did that administration really ever adopt an official definition? Do we have one under our current administration? I believe the answer to both questions is "no."

The following is a list of some operational and commonly used definitions or descriptions of terrorism that were used by the Reagan Administration:

> "the unlawful use or threatened use of force or violence by a revolutionary organization against individuals or property with the intention of coercing or intimidating governments or societies, often for political or ideological purposes."
>
> Department of Defense, 1983

> "violent criminal conduct apparently intended: (a) to intimidate or coerce a civilian population; (b) to influence the conduct of a government by intimidation or coercion, or (c) to affect the conduct of a government by assassination or kidnapping."
>
> Department of Justice, 1984

"the threat or use of violence for political purposes when (1) such action is intended to influence the attitude and behavior of a target group wider than its immediate victims, and (2) its ramifications transcend national boundaries."

CIA, 1978

"the unlawful use of force or violence against persons or property to intimidate or coerce a government, the civilian population, or any segment thereof, in furtherance of political or social objectives."

FBI, 1983

"premeditated [and] politically motivated violence perpetrated against noncombatant targets by subnational groups or clandestine state agents."

State Department, 1984

"the unlawful use or threat of violence against persons or property to further political or social objectives. It is usually intended to intimidate or coerce a government, individuals or groups or to modify their behavior or policies."

The Vice President's Task Force
on Combating Terrorism, 1986

We can see that the United States, as reported by Vice President Bush, did not have an adopted definition for terrorism, and that the agencies under the Reagan Administration all operated with different definitions.

In addition to this, there are different types or conceptions of terrorism as well:

(a) State terrorism:

Acts of terror perpetrated by governments using their own military or police forces. Examples are Nazi Germany, the slaughter of 20,000 Islamic fundamentalists by Syrian troops in Hama in 1982, and the widespread use of violence by several Latin American governments.

(b) State-sponsored terrorism:

> Support of quasi-independent terrorist groups by sympathetic governments. Support includes funds, training, arms, intelligence, or safe houses. Examples would include the Palestinian Saiqa organization (largely controlled by Syria) and the Salvadorean FMLN (which gets support from Cuba).

(c) Acts of war:

> Open military hostilities between governments, whether declared or not. Unlike terrorism, war usually avoids attacks on civilians and primarily involves conflicts between uniformed soldiers. Today, phrases such as "low intensity conflict" may be used to replace "war."

(d) Idiosyncratic terrorism:

> Disturbed individuals, acting without accomplices and without criminal or ideological motivation, can also terrorize. Examples include the San Ysidro, California, massacre at a MacDonald's restaurant in 1984, John Hinckley's attempted assassination of

President Reagan, and even the Oklahoma City Federal Building bombing by Timothy Mcveigh. Such acts are not however usually considered terrorism and may fall into the next category.

(e) Criminal acts:

A term reserved for acts of lawlessness where the motive is personal rather than ideological gain. Crime usually involves only the victim and the perpetrator. Terrorism involves a third party, the public. This distinction often becomes blurred in organized crime.

A Vice President's Report from George Bush Sr. has three categories of terrorism:

(1) Self-supported, which primarily rely on their own initiatives, such as extortion, kidnapping, bank robberies and narcotics trafficking to support their activities. This group tends to be extremely security conscious and remains small in numbers to avoid penetration.

(2) State-sponsored or aided, which are frequently large in numbers, has the advantage of protection by state

(3) agencies and are able to access state intelligence resources. It is extremely difficult to penetrate such groups.

(4) <u>Individuals</u> who engage in terrorism for limited tactical purposes. Some individuals or groups may choose to engage in terrorist violence in the context of activities such as national insurgency, especially when they may be losing a conflict, to try to create a special effect, embarrass opposing leadership, or change the pace of events.

The word "terrorist" appears to be a political term used by U.S. officials to describe opponents who engage in isolated violent attacks against the United States or its allies. Those who perform such acts, however, see themselves as "Freedom Fighters" against a vastly superior armed force or nation they believe is seeking to dominate or oppress them.

Modern "terrorist" attacks against the United States have not involved organized militia, but are hit and run raids that target a specific building, bridge, airport, plane, ship, or police/military barracks, with the USS Cole and September 11 attacks being two of the most recent examples.

The United States uses very similar terrorist attacks but instead describes them as "covert action," with the difference being intent. The CIA has been responsible for numerous such acts, and they are always instigated within a political context.

It is believed by many factions that the superiority of its military power and the arrogance that accompanies it make it possible for the United States to initiate such attacks on other countries while being the first to condemn similar actions taken by other nations against either U.S. allies or the United States itself. Such perceived hypocrisy fuels the flames or resentment against the United States.

The next logical step would be to list all of the many terrorist organizations, but it is more important to this discussion to understand which countries the Reagan Administration considered to be supporters of state-sponsored terrorism. These countries were Libya, Syria, Lebanon, Iran, Cuba, North Korea, and Nicaragua.

Replace Nicaragua with Iraq, and under the Clinton Administration these same countries were called "rogue states." This term was used to refer to those nations that oppose the foreign and military policies of the United States in their region, including U.S. actions and efforts to dominate those countries.

Most U.S. citizens accept the government's view on "rogue states" because the major news media parrot the Pentagon's point of view.

However, in nearly every case of suspected terrorism, the United States was in fact the original aggressor, using its own form of aggression to which the "rogue states" were responding.

Both Ambassador Oakley, in his address before the Conference on Terrorism on Feb. 13, 1986, and Vice President Bush, in his Report to the President, said that the Middle East had become the primary source of international terrorism.

Ambassador Oakley said that the Middle East had increased from 35% of the world terrorist incidents to 45% in 1985. Syria, Iran, Libya, and Lebanon support these organizations.

Currently, the United States is once again saying that the primary source of terrorism is the Middle East. Did the Reagan Doctrine help to curb terrorism? Will the current Administration do any better?

The reality is that many foreign terrorists actually learned their tactics from the CIA.

The most striking and ironic characteristic of the network financed and organized by Usama Bin Laden, the alleged master-mind of the September 11, 2001 attacks, is that it is made up almost entirely of Ronald Reagan's "Freedom Fighters," the Islamic fundamentalists armed and trained by the CIA in the 1980s in an effort to drive Soviet forces out of Afghanistan. This network received $6 billion in U.S. and Saudi-financed arms shipments in the 1980s.

Interestingly, Vice President Bush's report said that the majority of terrorist incidents in 1985, against Americans, occurred in Latin America. This had a significant impact on important foreign policy interests.

Americans were the number one target of international terrorist attacks in Latin America, and more incidents involving American persons or property took place there than in any other region.

Out of the twenty-eight major terrorist incidents involving U.S. citizens or property during the year prior to the raid, none were committed by Libyans, and only eight could really be claimed to have been committed by Libyan-backed individuals or assets.

Chapter 2

Reagan Administration's Policy on Terrorism

According to the Public Report by Vice President Bush, the U.S. position on terrorism is unequivocal: firm opposition to terrorism in all its forms and wherever it takes place.

The U.S. policy is based upon the conviction that to give into terrorists' demands places even more American lives at risk. *This no-concessions policy is the best way of ensuring the safety of the greatest number of people.* The following are statements by President Reagan and senior government officials on this U.S. policy:

- The U.S. Government is opposed to domestic and international terrorism and is prepared to act in concert with other nations or unilaterally when necessary to prevent or respond to terrorist acts.

- The U.S. Government considers the practice of terrorism by any person or group a potential threat to its national security and will resist the use of terrorism by all legal means available.

- States that practice terrorism or actively support it will not do so without consequence. If there is evidence that a state is mounting or intends to conduct an act of terrorism against this country, the United States will take measures to protect its citizens, property and interests.

- The U.S. Government will make no concessions to terrorists. It will not pay ransoms, release prisoners, change its policies or agree to other acts that might encourage additional terrorism. At the same time, the United States will use every available resource to gain the safe return of American citizens who are held hostage by terrorists.

- The United States will act in a strong manner against terrorists without surrendering basic freedoms or endangering democratic principles, and encourages other governments to take similar stands.

Moving from policy to organization, I begin by looking at the period following the attacks at the Munich Olympics, when President Nixon established a Cabinet-level committee, chaired by the Secretary of State, to combat terrorism. During the Carter Administration, a more responsive program coordinated by the National Security Council replaced this group.

During the first year of President Reagan's Administration, an organizational structure for crisis management was established with a group chaired by the Vice President and supported by appropriate interagency working groups.

In April 1982, President Reagan refined specific Lead Agency responsibilities for the coordination of the Federal response to terrorist incidents:

- Department of State - incidents that take place outside U.S. territory.

- Department of Justice (FBI) - incidents that take place within U.S. territory.

- Federal Aviation Administration (FAA) - incidents aboard aircraft that take place within the special jurisdiction of the United States.

In addition to the Lead Agency responsibilities, a number of interagency groups were established to facilitate coordination, including the Interdepartmental Group on Terrorism, to develop and coordinate overall U.S. policy on terrorism.

Chaired by the Department of State, the group met frequently to deal with issues such as international cooperation, research and development, legislation, public diplomacy, training programs and antiterrorist exercises.

Going back to policy, we need to look at the U.S. policy on responses to terrorism. According to the Reagan Administration, terrorism requires a coordinated national response on three levels.

First, the immediate problem of managing incidents must include measures taken before, during and after the event.

Second, coping with the threat is a long-term task that involves protecting people and property, reducing threat levels, and influencing the users and sponsors of terrorism to desist.

Finally, there is the challenge of identifying and alleviating the causes of terrorism.

The options for managing terrorist incidents by the Reagan Administration were:

- Preemption - Such actions were designed to keep an attack from occurring. Preemptive success is limited by the extent to which timely, accurate intelligence is available.

- Delay - Sometimes avoiding specific reactions until the circumstances are favorable is the best course. Delaying tactics are used during a terrorist incident in order to stall for time to position forces, keep the terrorists off balance, or develop other responses.

- Third-Party Arrangements - When incidents occur overseas the host country has primary responsibility for managing the situation. In other cases for diplomatic or political reasons, the use of third parties may offer the best opportunity for successful resolution of the incident.

- Negotiating - The United States has a clear policy of no concessions to terrorists as the best way to protect the greatest number of people. However, the United States Government has always stated that it will talk to anyone and use every available resource to gain the release of Americans held hostage.

- Counterattacking or Force Options - Forceful resolution of a terrorist incident can be risky. Careful planning and accurate, detailed intelligence are required to minimize risks.

The following were the Reagan Administration's considerations in determining responses to terrorism:

The United States can retaliate politically, economically, and militarily. The utility of these actions depends in great measure on cooperation from other countries, but they can have a positive, long-range deterrent effect.

Use of our well-trained and capable military forces offers an excellent chance of success if a military option can be implemented. Such use also demonstrates U.S. resolve to support stated

national policies. Military actions may serve to
deter future terrorist acts and could also
encourage other countries to take a harder line.
Successful employment however, depends on
timely and refined intelligence and prompt
positioning of forces.

Counter-terrorism missions are high-risk/high-
gain operations, which can have a severe
negative impact on U.S. prestige if they fail. A
U.S. military show of force may intimidate the
terrorists and their sponsors and would not
immediately risk more U.S. lives or prestige and
could be more effective if utilized in concert
with diplomatic, political or economic sanctions.

There are however, some distinct disadvantages:
a show of force could be considered gunboat
diplomacy, which might be perceived as a
challenge rather than a credible threat; it may
require a sizable deployment of support
activities; it may provide our enemies with a
subject for anti-American propaganda
campaigns worldwide; and most important, an
active military response may be necessary to
resolve the situation if a show of force fails.

For the purpose of future discussions, one more aspect of the Reagan
Administration's policies that ties into terrorism needs to be included--
Executive Order 12333 discusses assassination:

2.11 Prohibition on Assassination. No person employed by or acting on behalf of the United States Government shall engage in, or conspire to engage in, assassination.

2.12 Indirect Participation. No agency of the intelligence community shall participate in or request any person to undertake activities forbidden by this order.

What has been discussed in this chapter is the "official" policy of the Reagan Administration. Keep this in mind as we discuss actual world events in further chapters.

Chapter 3

Reagan Administration Foreign Policy

In order to explore alternative explanations, other than terrorism for the United States bombing of Libya, we need to look at the Reagan Administration's foreign policy in general. To be more specific, we need to look into the Reagan idea of "American Image," the foreign policy toward other state sponsored terrorist countries, and patterns in his decision-making process that make the raid uncharacteristic with the Administration's normal response to terrorism.

Successful presidents are all alike, while each failure fails in their own way. Warren Harding, Herbert Hoover, and Jimmy Carter did not fail the same way as Lyndon Johnson and Richard Nixon, but each damaged the country.

By contrast, the best ones, Washington, Jackson, Lincoln, the Roosevelts, the early Cold War presidents, and yes, Ronald Reagan, all shared some pertinent traits: all were able to define and embody the national purpose and character, to name the key challenges of their era and meet those challenges.

Two things conspired to make Reagan special:

> First, he came from the entertainment world, not business, the law, or the military; and no one before had thought of the film studios as a breeding ground for future world leaders.

> Second, he reached power at a time when the traits shared by all the great American leaders of the past--a fierce patriotism, a keen moral sense, and an ease with and wish to use power--were no longer in style with the chattering classes, and were even considered outré and sinister.

Reagan understood power and knew how to use it to achieve results. He was also a visionary, who knew how to feed imagination into calculations of power. Some believe you have to work around reality, Reagan wanted to change reality itself.

Ronald Reagan's "American Image" and Reagan foreign policy are related, but conceptually different. One is an idea, the other is actions to carry out that idea.

President Reagan is the most ideologically oriented president to have occupied the White House in the post-World War II era. The image that was foremost in everything Reagan did was the projection of American strength. Time will tell however, if the current Bush Administration will surpass this ideology.

After taking over from Carter, Reagan's main effort was to show America as a world power once again, and his foreign policy was based on this concept. Power was a crucial factor in Reagan's world of politics, and was probably the single most important element in determining the course of international interactions. As part of his "American Image," Reagan used both "real power" and "perceived power" in the international arena. By this I mean that Reagan let the world know that the United States had the *capacity* to enforce policy, and that his Administration had the *will*.

There are numerous political scientists that will say that for the first few years in office Reagan did not have an identifiable foreign policy.

Others, such as Philip Geyelin, say, "It is arguable whether, for Mr. Reagan, the world ever ceases to be a stage. Perhaps it doesn't, and perhaps that is the point; Mr. Reagan's approach to foreign policy over the years, and his performance in the first six years of his presidency in particular, have defied conventional or orthodox tests and standards applied by foreign policy practitioners, historians and academics."

There appeared to be no "rock bottom" to Reagan's political power in foreign policy: it rested almost wholly on public faith in the image of the President and all the good things he symbolized (America Standing Tall), rather than on the firm foundation of unsentimental support for his policies, his programs and his performance.

An important point to remember when trying to understand the Reagan thought-process is to understand that Reagan, a kind man in his personal relationships, could not seem to understand that many of his critics were evaluating the results of his policies rather than his motivations.

Globalism, anti-communism, and containment, with the Soviet Union being the single most threat to the United States and the world, was the main thrust of the Reagan foreign policy once one was established. Almost every time Reagan made a speech he would talk about his image of America, the image of strength, and of its role in the world as the guardian of world peace.

Just one example of this is President Reagan's televised address to the nation on Feb 26, 1986, where he made the following comment, "My fellow Americans, I want to speak to you this evening about my highest duty as President--to preserve the peace and defend these United States."

"*To be prepared for war is one of the most effective ways of preserving peace.*" George Washington's words may seem hard and cold today, but history has proven him right again and again. The past year or so has shown that American strength is once again a sheltering arm for freedom in a dangerous world.

Strength is the most persuasive argument we have to convince our adversaries to negotiate seriously and to cease bullying other nations. American power is the indispensable element of a peaceful world.

The foreign policy of the Reagan Administration encompassed not only the rebuilding of military capabilities, but also a rebirth of the American spirit in place of the national self-doubt of the Vietnam era.

In the early 1980s, two contrasting basic approaches to American strategy asserted themselves.   The "*Peripheral Strategy*" called for military capabilities based principally on strategic-nuclear forces, air power, and maritime supremacy, with a substantial emphasis on the assumption of greater defense burdens by allies.

The other approach, the "*Continental Strategy,*" or forward defense concept, stressed the need for the United States, with a balanced-force posture, to maintain substantial ground forces both in Europe and Asia as a means of countering superior numbers of mobilized Soviet capabilities and of preserving deterrence.

The Reagan Administration needed to define the limits of American foreign policy in a dynamic and rapidly changing global security environment and, above all, to relate its international commitments to existing and prospective capabilities in a fashion acceptable to the electorate.

While devoting greater resources to defense, the Reagan Administration sought to evolve a national consensus for the conduct of foreign policy. Illustrative of this was the formation of a series of criteria for the future use of military power.

In 1984 it was asserted by the Administration that the United States should be guided by six criteria in any decision to commit forces to combat areas:

> (1) the engagement should be clearly in the national interest;

> (2) the commitment should be wholehearted, with the clear intention of achieving victory;

> (3) political and military objectives should be precisely identified, with an appropriate strategy for using committed forces to attain them;

> (4) there must be a continuing reassessment of the relationship between means and ends after forces have been sent into action;

> (5) there must be a strong likelihood of support from both the American people and Congress;

and the utilization of U.S. military power in
combat should be only a last resort.

The foreign policy of the Reagan Administration was always
presented in a very polished manner to the American people as being one
of American strength and consistency, but in reality it was one of
countless problems and inconsistencies.

Early in the Reagan presidency, complaints were heard that Secretary
of Defense Casper Weinberger was functioning as the de facto Secretary
of State; that the foreign policy of the Reagan Administration lacked
"predictability and coherence;" that statements by Secretary of State
Alexander Haig did not really represent the viewpoints of the president;
and that "open political combat" had erupted among the president's
advisers on relations with the Soviet Union and other major foreign
policy questions.

Even after Secretary of State Haig's resignation, and his replacement
by George Shultz, disunity continued to prevail among officials in the
executive branch on several key foreign policy issues. In its efforts to
stabilize the Middle East, for example, the Reagan Administration's
viewpoints were confused by the somewhat contradictory statements of
Secretary Shultz and Defense Secretary Casper Weinberger concerning
the role of American armed forces in enforcing any peace agreement
reached.

Similar confusion about the nature of the challenge and America's
proper response to it marked the Administration's approach to
revolutionary turmoil in Latin America.

A public opinion poll taken in 1983 showed that only 35% of those
responding believed that President Reagan was "in control" of the
Executive branch. These are just some examples that show what was

going on behind the scenes while the American people were believing that the Administration knew what it was doing and had a strong, firm foreign policy.

With the benefit of hindsight, President Reagan's performance in the White House does not lend itself to easy interpretation. The study of presidential personality and character "at a distance" is difficult, especially in a case where the correspondence between a president's words and his actions are loosely knit.

Reagan has been enigmatic, because his statements and actions have often been inconsistent. It has been difficult to disentangle the rhetoric of Reagan "the actor" from the convictions of Reagan the decider.

Reagan is characterized as a "nice guy, Teflon president." His desires to be liked and to be a hero were overriding. But it was his theatrical talents that enabled him to avoid paying the political costs for his often excessive efforts to imbue the foreign policy of the United States with his personal convictions.

Reagan's errors did not stick to his presidency, nonetheless, he stands as a classic crusader. Reagan's foreign policy was based on deeply held ideological convictions, of these, the most important was anti-communism...Communism [to Reagan] was still a monolithic evil force that would bully, lie, and cheat its way to world conquest.

During his first term, Reagan did not try to correct this image with new facts, but surrounded himself with like minded-men. Ronald Reagan's shallow knowledge of history and foreign policy snared him into several serious mistakes.

From the beginning, the Reagan Administration continually reaffirmed its commitment to an activist internationalist posture where the primary tool to be used was the military. Priority was given to projecting American power abroad, to demonstrating the nation's resolve to retain its global influence, to protecting its interest everywhere, and to tightening the American grip on developments worldwide.

At this point we should note the affects of the so-called Reagan Doctrine on the operation of American foreign policy. The Doctrine sought to take American foreign policy beyond the confines of the Truman Doctrine to the next logical level: U.S. policy would no longer merely defend states threatened by communist insurgency, it would now actively assist anti-Communist "freedom fighters" everywhere. The anticipated result being to discredit, or even overthrow, the present regime.

In principle, the Reagan Doctrine was universal in scope, but in practice it was selective. According to the Reagan Doctrine, the way to help democratic countries was by bringing down those radical regimes that Reagan thought were a puppet of the Soviet Union and therefore a threat to democratic countries.

Reagan's total commitment was to thwart Soviet expansion, and although the United States could not assume global responsibility for all regional and local disputes, the Reagan Administration's strategic approach to foreign policy had as a principle premise that no region lies beyond American interest if control or influence by a hostile power threatens the security of the U.S.

The Reagan Philosophy represented a radical departure from the foreign policy of the previous decade. Presidents Nixon, Ford, and Carter had consistently, although in different ways, conducted foreign policies that were adjusting to the changing world. Each pursued an active diplomacy to compensate for the diffusion of international power that had become so evident by the late 1960's. Reagan reversed the logic by the belief that Washington's policies should not have to adjust to the world, but that a strong assertive America could make the world adjust.

The Administration would try to undermine the regimes it defined as radical by assisting the opposition in overthrowing the current leadership, conducting CIA covert operations, including assassination attempts, and engaging in direct military actions.

Examples of radical regimes that Reagan attempted to topple are Angola, Nicaragua, Cuba, and North Korea. What they all had in common was their relationship with the Soviet Union.

The interesting part about Reagan's attitude toward Libya is that when Reagan first took office, the Libyans were not pro-Soviet, but as mounting pressure from the U.S. increased, the Libyans even told the Reagan Administration that if they continued on their current path to overthrow the Libyan leadership, they would have no alternative but to go to the Soviet Union for support. This suggests the possibility that the Reagan Administration purposely pushed the Libyan leadership toward the Soviet Union so that it would be easier to justify future U.S. actions.

President Reagan considered Syria, Cuba, Iran, and Nicaragua to be just as bad, or worse, than Libya when it came to sponsoring international terrorism; and yet the U.S. policy toward them did not result in an air raid.

The U.S. imposed numerous economic and political sanctions against Syria because of its support of terrorism, the British government ordered the expulsion of diplomats when they had evidence of their involvement in terrorism, the Italian high court claimed to have positive proof of Syrian involvement in international terrorism, the West German government expelled three Syrian diplomats for terrorist involvement, and Canada withdrew its ambassador from Syria.   The Reagan Administration rattled the saber and made an appropriate amount of noise and chose to ignore the evidence available.

The Administration was taking every opportunity to make a big issue of any Libyan related involvement and to downplay any Syrian involvement, even though certain officials in the Administration said that, "Syria's involvement in terrorism was much more professional, and much more deadly than Libya's."

On Oct. 25, the U.S. even announced that it would withdraw its ambassador to Syria as support for the British. The Administration had a similar policy toward Iran even though they also were considered to be a major sponsor of international terrorism and a vocal enemy of the United States.

In 1984 Iran was classified by U.S. officials as one of the most active supporters of international terrorism. On July 8, 1985, President Reagan placed Iran at the top of the list of terrorist states. He charged, "In 1983 alone, the CIA either confirmed or found strong evidence of Iranian involvement in 47 terrorist attacks ... since Sept 1984, Iranian backed terrorist groups have been responsible for almost 30 attacks."

At this point the issue surrounding the sale of arms to Iran needs to be mentioned because it shows an inconsistency and a violation of the Administration's own policies discussed earlier.   The scandal that enveloped the Reagan administration in late 1986 was initially looked at by many as being similar to President Nixon's Watergate scandal.

Although the nation was clearly unwilling to go through such an ordeal again so soon, President Reagan remained personally popular, even though according to polls taken, most Americans thought he was not being truthful about his involvement.

Nevertheless the abuses of power by the Reagan Administration were considered more serious than those of Nixon because of their effects on U.S. foreign policy. Through the National Security Council, the White House had organized a "shadow government" that secretly sold arms to Iran to gain the release of six U.S. hostages held in Lebanon in violation of the Arms Export Control Act banning arms shipments to states that sponsored terrorism (which had been applied to Iran by a Reagan executive order).

The Reagan administration also violated a requirement to notify Congressional intelligence committees if the president authorized covert arms sales. It further established a network of private individuals, mostly former government officials, some of rather unsavory reputation (because of their earlier association with Edmond Wilson, who had supplied Libya's Colonel Qaddafi with terrorist capabilities, including arms and training by former Special Forces personnel), as well as foreign personnel, including Iranian, Saudi, and Israeli arms dealers. It employed these men as agents of the U.S. government to carry out an arms-for-hostages exchange with Iran. It then used some of the profits from this deal to supply arms to the U.S., and organized and supported Contras against the Nicaraguan government.

As revelations of these activities surfaced in November 1986, the White House and NSA, together with the director of the CIA and the attorney general, attempted a cover-up by constructing a false chronology of events to protect the president by minimizing his role.

Reagan changed his story about when he first learned of the initial secret shipment of U.S. arms to Iran via Israel in September 1985 and about whether he had authorized it to gain the release of the U.S. hostages. He claimed a loss of memory on this radical shift of policy from his own earlier and repeated insistence that the United States would never deal with terrorists.

From the beginning of his administration, Reagan vowed to deal firmly with terrorists, whether sponsored by states like Iran or not. His administration claimed they would not bargain with terrorists because that would only encourage further acts of terrorism.

But as terrorist acts multiplied throughout the Middle East and Europe, the administration remained passive. The exception was the bombing of Libya, which did not make a lot of sense in the fight against terrorism when taking the overall picture of world events during this time period into account.

Even after the administration's arms-for-hostages deal with Iran, only one hostage was released after each of three shipments, and three more hostages were seized in Lebanon. It was clear that the Administration's decision to trade arms for hostages gave the terrorists an incentive to replace the ones released.

Quite apart from not gaining all the hostages' freedom and violating U.S. laws, the Reagan Administration exposed itself as hypocritical and undermined its own tough antiterrorist public posture of never surrendering to terrorist blackmail. It sanctioned the usual European approach of bartering for hostages and undermined the British effort to lead Europe to adopt Reagan's publicly stated position of not dealing with terrorists.

When we look back at Reagan's "American Image" and his "policy" on terrorism that supposedly was the reason he ordered the raid on Libya, then it is hard to understand how the President could place the lives of a few individuals over America's broader and longer-run national interests.

At the very least, it jeopardized the nation's--and his own--authority, reputation, and credibility at home and abroad.

To trade arms in a war (Iraq/Iran) in which it is against America's national interest for Iran to win, and to do so in a way that would encourage further hostage taking--all this with a regime that had only recently mocked and humiliated the United States and who had a hand in blowing up over 200 American Marines and diplomats in Lebanon-- raises serious questions about President Reagan's judgment and competence and the whole manner in which the Reagan Administration formulated and conducted policy.

It is clear that the Reagan Administration was not concerned with terrorism per se. The terrorism that most concerned the Administration was that attributed to Soviet proxies and surrogates; thus, fighting terrorism essentially meant fighting worldwide communism and Soviet influence.

The Reagan Administration chose to view nearly every international development through the prism of anti-communist ideology; every event that threatened to disturb the global status quo was traced to the revolutionary activities of a supposedly coordinated communist movement.

Whether an uprising of the left against their oppressors or rightist terrorism by nationalists pursuing national causes, the interpretation was the same: communism was responsible.

According to Reagan's Doctrine it was America's obligation to do more than just contain communism, it must eliminate it. From this stance, it was a short step to accepting repressive regimes that denied freedom to their own people but voiced opposition to Marxist principles. Thus Administration spokesmen in the early 1980s dismissed the denial of basic rights to people in South Africa, Argentina, Chile, the Philippines, Haiti, El Salvador, and elsewhere as beyond the purview of American concern.

Dictators were once again embraced by the United States. The message was clear to the dictators and tyrants of the world that if you claim to be anti-communist, the Reagan Administration would not give you any trouble.

Another example of the inconsistency of the Reagan foreign policy is identified by analyzing U.S.-Latin America foreign policy. If Reagan ordered the bombing of Libya for the reasons given, then why did he not order the invasion of Nicaragua?

On numerous occasions, President Reagan made public statements making it very clear that Nicaragua was the worst threat to the United States, and that it housed terrorist organizations. Yet the response did not support the claimed U.S. policy stated for the Libyan raid. Examples include:

> "My fellow Americans, I must speak to you tonight about a mounting danger in Central America that threatens the security of the United States. This danger will not go away; it will grow worse, much worse, if we fail to take action now. I am speaking of Nicaragua, a Soviet ally on the American mainland only two hours flying time from our boarders...gathered in Nicaragua already are thousands of Cuban military advisers, contingents of Soviets and East Germans, and all elements of international terror from the PLO to Italy's Red Brigades. Why are they there? Because as Colonel Qaddafi has publicly exulted: 'Nicaragua means

a great thing, it means fighting America near its borders--fighting America at its doorstep.' For our own security, the United States must deny the Soviet Union a beachhead in North America."

(Address by President Reagan, March 16, 1986)

"...Nicaragua today is an imprisoned nation. It is a nation condemned to unrelenting cruelty by a clique of very cruel men--by a dictator in designer glasses and his comrades, drunk with power and all its brutal applications... The truth is, these men are nothing but thugs, a gang of hardcore communists to whom the word God is a declaration that must be stamped out. Their denial of rights, their trampling of human dignity, their wrecking of an economy with suffocating socialist controls--all hurt and deeply offend us. But there is a cause for deeper concern: the specter of Nicaragua transformed into an international aggressor nation, a base for subversion and terror. ...terror groups are turning Managua into a breeding ground for subversion. ...And Nicaragua's connection with the recent terrorist attack against Columbia's

Supreme Court is now clear. What are we to
do about such aggressions? The answer is
more than we are doing now."

(President Reagan's address to the nation
Nov 23, 1985)

The Administration, determined to prevent a "second Cuba" in this
hemisphere and with the "first Cuba" on the mainland and convinced that
the Sandinistas were committed to a revolution without frontiers, would
seek to undermine not only El Salvador but other Central American
countries.   The administration committed itself to the support of the
Contras. The president rather generously called their leaders (Contras)
the "moral equals of our Founding Fathers."

Central America was seen as part of the East-West struggle with the
Administration being convinced that U.S security was at stake in
Nicaragua.   Besides SDI, there was no issue about which President
Reagan felt more strongly.

Another example of the Administration's inconsistent pattern in
decision-making and foreign policy was its dealings with South Africa.
The Reagan approach to South Africa was another exception to the
pattern of behavior shown in other cases.   Here, the Administration
pursued a policy of diplomatic engagement not only with South Africa
but also with its neighbors who had proclaimed Marxist ideologies (the
same ideology that the Administration claimed was so wrong in
Nicaragua).

U.S. diplomats were very active in pursuing a settlement in Namibia,
although with little evident progress, and improved relations between

Pretoria and its neighbors with apparent results in the achievement of a non-aggression pact between South Africa and Mozambique, and a cease fire between South Africa and Angola along the Namibian border.

This activism is not the only difference between this case and the others. While there was, again, resort to the use of 'sticks'—not directly, but in taking a neutral position on South Africa's use of force against its neighbors, there was also the provision of 'carrots.'

After the pact was signed, Reagan for the first time submitted a waiver to Congress and announced an economic assistance program for Mozambique, in addition to generous emergency food supplies. At the beginning of 1985 it went further, requesting $1 million from Congress for non-lethal military aid.

The point is that there was remarkably little concern about the ideological makeup of the Angolan and Mozambique governments. Despite these regimes' espousal of radical philosophies, Secretary of State Shultz met with the Angolan Interior Minister in April 1983, and in July the Administration restored relations with Mozambique to the Ambassadorial level.

To be sure, the Administration was sympathetic to Jonas Savimbi and his guerrillas in their struggle against the Angolan government. They refused recognition of the Angolan government, and wished to see Mozambique join the International Monetary Fund in order to encourage its pragmatic moves away from a government-directed economy. But in general, the Administration pursued its diplomacy without letting ideological differences bar professional exchanges in views.

Why had such policies as those previously discussed been pursued in South Africa and not in Nicaragua? The question, not the answer, is what is important to the issue at hand.

Chapter 4

Confrontations Between the U.S. and Libya/Qaddafi

This chapter will concentrate its focus of discussion on Libya, the attitude of the Reagan administration toward Qaddafi and the political and economic pressures leading up to the raid.

The hostility experienced both then and today between the United States and Iran is the result of five decades of U.S. interference. For example, there was the CIA-supported overthrow of Iran's Prime Minister, Mohammad Mossadegh, in 1953, the disintegration of U.S.–Iran relations during the Carter administration, and our hoisting of Western values and policies on that country, which eventually led to the fundamentalist takeover and the resultant hostage crisis in 1979.

Another example of U.S. terrorist tactics occurred when Israel invaded Lebanon in June 1982. The Reagan administration stationed U.S. Marines at the Beirut airport and engaged in the naval bombardment of Muslim-held areas in Beirut, killing Lebanese civilians. This was the context in April 1983 that prompted the truck bomb attack that killed 241 Marines and the bombing of the U.S. embassy in Beirut. A Pentagon board of inquiry, headed by Admiral L. J. Long, strongly condemned Ronald Reagan's policy in Lebanon that had led to the terrorism against the Marines and the embassy.

Reagan and his advisers were also responsible for the U.S. fleet attack on Libya in March 1986 that killed sixty Libyan sailors and the April bombing of Libyan cities that killed and injured hundreds of civilians.

In addition, according to the April 16, 1986, New York Times, the Pentagon's "precision bombing" of Tripoli damaged the embassies of France, Austria, and Rumania, the residences of Swiss and Japanese Ambassadors, as well as the Bin Ashun neighborhood of the Libyan middle class and intelligencia.

The following are significant terrorist incidents involving Americans in the year prior to the raid on Libya:

Jan 30,   Guadalajara, Mexico:

An American and his Cuban friend were taken from a restaurant and killed.

Feb 2,   Glyfada, Greece:

A bomb exploded in a nightclub frequented by U.S. military personnel. A group called the "National Front" claimed the bombing was in protest of U.S. support for Turkey over the Cyprus issue.

Feb 7, Guadalajara, Mexico:

A DEA agent was abducted and killed after leaving the U.S. consulate.

Feb 7, Medellin, Columbia:

Terrorists simultaneously bombed seven establishments, most of which were U.S. firms. The Che Guevara Faction of the National Liberation Army and the Ricardo Franco Front claimed responsibility.

Feb 21, Barranquilla, Columbia:

A bomb exploded outside of the Bi-national Center.

Apr 9, Santiago, Chile:

Two explosive devices detonated in a shopping arcade. At the same time five other bombs exploded in four other cities in Chile.

<u>Apr 12, Madrid, Spain:</u>

A bomb exploded in the El Descanso restaurant, which was frequented by U.S. military personnel from a nearby air base. Several groups, including the Islamic Jihad organization, claimed responsibility.

<u>May 15, Lima, Peru:</u>

Simultaneous bombings occurred at a number of targets in the city, including the residence of the U.S. Ambassador.

<u>June 14, Beirut, Lebanon:</u>

TWA Flight 847 from Athens to Beirut was hijacked with 153 passengers on board. Lebanese Shi'ites were responsible.

<u>June 19, San Salvador, El Salvador:</u>

Gunmen shot and killed 13 people, including four Marine Embassy Guards, at an outdoor cafe. The Marines, who were in civilian clothes, were singled out. The Revolutionary Party of Central American Workers claimed credit.

June 23, Air India Flight 182:

Flying from Toronto and Montreal to India, Flight 182 crashed at sea off southwest Ireland as a result of an explosion. All 329 passengers died. The Sikh group claimed credit.

July 1, Madrid, Spain:

Terrorists attacked a building shared by TWA and British Airways. The Abu Nidal group claimed credit.

July 1, Andori, Columbia:

Attackers, believed to be with the leftist National Liberation Army, shot and severely wounded Douglas Brannen, a former Florida State senator.

July 14, Karachi, Pakistan:

A bomb exploded near the main entrance of a Pan Am office. No group claimed credit.

July 19, Santiago, Chile:

A powerful car bomb exploded in front of the U.S. Consulate. The Manual Rodriguez Patriotic Front claimed credit.

July 22, Copenhagen, Denmark:

Two bomb blasts wrecked the offices of Northwest Orient and damaged a Jewish Synagogue and old people's home. The Islamic Jihad took credit.

Aug 7, Wiesbaden, West Germany:

A U.S. serviceman was shot, killed, and robbed of his military ID card after leaving a night club. The Red Army Faction used the ID card for the bombing at a U.S. air base the next day.

Aug 8, Frankfurt, West Germany:

A car bomb exploded in a parking lot at the U.S. Rhein-Main Air Base. The Red Army Faction claimed credit.

Sept 3, Cali, Columbia:

A large bomb exploded in the library of the U.S.-Columbian Bi-national Center, and three bombs were placed in front of the Coca-Cola bottling plant. Both the M-19 and the Ricardo Franco Front claimed responsibility.

Sept 9, Madrid, Spain:

A car bomb exploded in central Madrid during rush hour. ETA, a Basque separatist group, claimed responsibility.

Sept 16, Rome, Italy:

Two Soviet-made grenades were thrown into the Cafe de Paris, a popular tourist spot located 100 yards from the U.S. Embassy. The Abu Nidal group claimed responsibility.

Oct 7, Port Said, Egypt:

For gunmen seized the Italian cruise ship Achille Lauro off Port Said, Egypt. The hijackers killed a wheelchair bound American hostage and threw his body overboard.

Oct 23, Concepcion, Chile:

A bomb exploded at the U.S.-Chilean Bi-national Center. The Manuel Rodriguez Patriotic Front claimed responsibility.

Oct 28, Santiago, Chile:

Bombs exploded at the offices of two U.S. companies.

Nov 6, San Juan, Puerto Rico:

Major Michael Snyder, a U.S. Army recruiting officer was shot and wounded on his way to work. The Organization of Volunteers for the Puerto Rican Revolution claimed responsibility.

Nov 23, Malta:

An Egyptian flight carrying 96 people was highjacked en route from Athens to Cairo and diverted to Malta by three Arab speaking gunmen. When demands for refueling were not met two Israeli women and three Americans were shot in the head. Three groups claimed responsibility: Egypt's Revolution, The Egyptian Liberation Organization, and the Abu Nidal group.

Nov 24, Frankfurt, West Germany:

A car bomb exploded at a U.S. military post exchange. No group claimed credit.

Dec 27, Rome, Italy; Vienna, Austria:

Terrorists simultaneously attacked passengers at airports in Rome and Vienna with grenades and automatic weapons. The Abu Nidal group claimed credit for the attack.

When Reagan assumed the presidency in 1981, Libyan officials expressed some hope that there might be a positive change in the American position toward the Arab-Israeli conflict. Qaddafi believed Republicans to be more sympathetic toward the Arabs than the Democrats.

Qaddafi sent a letter to President Reagan on January 27, 1981, asking him for an unbiased American stand toward the conflict. "On this occasion we call on America, under your administration, to play a different role, respecting the will of peoples and ending oppressive U.S. intervention, both covert and overt, in the international affairs of other countries."

Qaddafi asserted that "the Libyan Arab people look forward to sound and equitable relations based on mutual respect and interests." But the new Administration was under the conviction that Libya was a proxy of the Soviets.

This conviction was heavily reinforced by Sadat in Egypt and Numeiry in Sudan, who warned that Libya's role in Chad was to expand Soviet influence and destabilize other African regimes friendly to the West. So the Reagan Administration started in its early days, to follow an aggressive/hostile policy toward Libya.

The Libyan officials' reaction was first to point out that those claims were untrue and that Libya was an independent nonaligned country. In a speech on January 21, 1981, Qaddafi reaffirmed that argument:

> "The Americans realize that the Libyan presence in Chad is purely Libyan and they know the reasons behind it. They also know that Libya is an independent and neutral state, neither Marxist nor Communist and it is not under the Soviet Union's influence, and that there are no Soviet bases on Libyan soil.... If as Sadat raves day and night that there are Soviet bases in Libya, the Americans would laugh at what he says because the Americans possess spy satellites and know what is going out of or into the Soviet Union."

The aggressive/hostile U.S. approach toward Libya did not stop, and Libya went back to its militant anti-American policy, condemning the U.S. "imperial" policy in the region and attacking all the reactionary Arab regimes such as Egypt, Sudan, Somalia, and Saudi Arabia.

To Libyan officials, as stated by Qaddafi on May 14, 1981, "The new U.S. Administration has proven that it is more stupid than the Carter Administration and has no idea what international politics is all about."

This resulted in Libya leaning more toward the Soviet Union, which was emphasized in a statement by the Libyan government in May 1981, "Libya is a neutral country, but U.S. pressures do not help it to remain neutral and could force it to become completely pro-Soviet."

In addition to this tactical approach, Libya was still trying to show its readiness for dialogue and compromise. This readiness was reflected in a June 1981 visit by a high level Libyan official to Washington to meet with U.S. officials and members of Congress to clarify what was believed to be a misperceived Libyan policy.

The meeting did not bring about any concrete results.   Widely published reports during the summer of 1981 that the CIA had articulated a plan to get rid of the Libyan leader caused a more extreme reaction which started the open threats by Libya toward the American leadership and people.

In August 1981, Libya sent a note to the Security Council charging that the United States was making preparations to attack Libya militarily, and on August 17 Libya signed a friendship treaty with Ethiopia and South Yemen, pledging to combat the "imperial influence" in the area. This treaty was seen by the U.S. as a threat to American interests in East Africa and the Indian Ocean, and Libya was seen as attempting to undermine Numeiry's regime in Sudan.

Even as late as September 1981, Libya still tried to establish normal relations with the United States but said one of the main obstacles to normal relations was President Reagan himself, who was perceived as a liar, silly, and ignorant.

In one of his statements, Qaddafi characterized Reagan as follows: "He was born to be an insignificant and unsuccessful actor; all his acting dealt with the smuggling of funds outside America. How could he become the president of the greatest state on earth? What a comedy--the comedy of the 20th Century, the absurdity of the 20th Century, the triviality of the 20th Century."

Throughout 1982 the situation remained about the same with the Libyans trying to maintain relations with the U.S. and at the same time reacting to the American squeeze.

By the end of 1982, Qaddafi's assessment of Reagan changed slightly, which was apparent in his statement that, "He has changed a little, no doubt. At first, he was a 100 percent ignoramus as far as international relations are concerned. Today, he grasps at least 25 percent of the world problems."

Qaddafi's master plan of today is a significantly expanded version of the concept that drove him to seek power in Libya from the beginning. In Qaddafi's view, the ultimate purpose of the Libyan revolution of September 1, 1969, was to begin the process of Arab unification.

Starting with the neighboring states of Tunis, Algeria, Niger, Chad, and Sudan, Qaddafi began a process of destabilization through the revival of long standing boundary disputes. Writing in the September 1980 issue of Afrique, Souhel Aziz notes that for purposes of achieving his primary aims, Qaddafi has divided Africa north of the equator into three distinct but complementary geopolitical zones.

Zone 1 constitutes the region of sub-Saharan Africa;

Zone 2, the Maghreb;

Zone 3, the Saharan "belt" stretching between zone 1 and 2 along an axis from Nouakchott (Mauritania) to N'Djamena (Chad), and passing through Bamako (Mali) and Niamey (Niger).

Without going into all of the data surrounding the Libyan plan for Africa, we must realize that the stakes in Africa were far too high to believe that the Reagan Administration allowed itself to get distracted by Libyan state sponsored terrorism.

Libyan terrorism was nothing compared to the problems for American interests that Libya was causing in Africa. But, as a whole, American people were emotional about the subject of terrorism and knew very little and could care less about the problems in Africa.

In addition to this, there was Libya's deep involvement with Nicaragua, Cuba, North Korea, Syria, Lebanon, the August 14 announcement of the union between Libya and Morocco, and the reports of nuclear weapons potential, all of which probably concerned the U.S. more than the issue of terrorism.

Now we will look at the Reagan Administrations policy, attitude, and actions toward Libya.

The election of Ronald Reagan to the U.S. presidency as mentioned earlier, produced a dramatic shift in the Libyan-U.S. relationship. Once in office, the Reagan Administration systematically increased the military, diplomatic, and economic pressure on Libya in an effort to isolate it internationally and promote the downfall of the Qaddafi government.

Qaddafi, inaccurately labeled a Soviet puppet, was characterized as an international rogue who had to be controlled if not replaced. In a little over a year, U.S. foreign policy toward Libya had been fundamentally altered. The U.S. government had come to recognize Qaddafi, not as simply an irritant or nuisance, but as an enemy.

There was a fairy tale that American policymakers used to believe during the Eisenhower Administration that was revived among the Reagan Administration officials. It was a fairy tale about the Arabs and how the U.S. should deal with them.

Once upon a time, according to this story, there were two kinds of Arabs. Good Arabs and bad Arabs. The good Arabs were the ones who would do exactly what the United States wanted if Washington gave them rewards. The bad Arabs are the ones who refuse to do exactly what Washington wants, no matter what rewards they are offered.

The "baddest" Arab of them all was, of course, Qaddafi. Being a "bad" Arab according to this (Reagan) thought process only causes U.S. rewards to dry up; it invites punishments for the "bad" Arab country's economy, encouragement to internal opponents, and assassination plots.

What both Arabs have in common, according to Washington policymakers, is that being Arabs, they have an obligation to take orders from Washington. While Washington had many reasons to support this thought process, it fundamentally meant that the Arab world was too important to the United States and Western interests to allow Arab self-determination and independence.

The initial approach of the Reagan Administration toward Libya was in some ways similar to its Nicaraguan policies. Just as Nicaragua was used to dramatize the threat in Central America and the difference in approach from that of the Carter years, so Libya and its leader were used to demonstrate both the threat of international terrorism, and again the contrast of Carter's policies.

As time went on, the Reagan Administration became more and more openly hostile toward Libya as it stood up to the Administration. Ronald Reagan called Qaddafi names like "the most dangerous man in the world," "barbaric," "flaky," "pariah," and a "mad dog."

Secretary of State George Shultz, architect of strategy against Libya, declared: "We have to put Qaddafi in a box and close the lid."

Chester Crocker, Assistant Secretary of State for Africa, has claimed that Qaddafi is "probably the most disastrous source of destabilization in Africa."

In the early hours of an April morning in 1986, fighter-bombers of the U.S. Air Force, streaking from their bases in the United Kingdom, reaffirmed an idea espoused by General Billy Mitchell almost 60 years earlier: bombs dropped from aircraft can take out specific targets. The results in the 1920s and in 1986 were the same, but the circumstances and hardware changed considerably.

Technology has taken us from clear weather, to all-weather, day-or-night, pinpoint-accuracy bombing, providing the destructive force of a 500-pound bomb, or an area weapon that can be targeted to meet your definition of "pinpoint."

Technology allowed us the latitude to expand exponentially the means used to fight.

We fly great distances at great speeds and deliver tons of ordnance with an efficiency that Billy Mitchell would not have dreamed of, although what is now reality is certainly an extension of his dream. In the end, we accomplish what he did with biplanes at 120 knots--we destroy a target. This is air power, and the essence of air power's strength is the ability to destroy an enemy's physical means to resist by destroying selected targets.

Air power also provides the flexibility to achieve objectives that range from the limited to the broad. The achievement of a broad objective, however, is really an amalgam of limited objectives.

Putting bombs on target is therefore closely allied with the choice of targets and tactical planning, which in turn are based on the scope of objectives chosen and on the decision to employ armed force.

In the limited sense, if we say that air power in a certain instance, we should mean that the bombs did not hit the target. An example is the Thanh Hoa Bridge in North Vietnam.

When F-105 aircraft could not destroy the bridge in the mid-1960s, it could be said that, in the limited sense, air power failed and that when the bridge fell in 1972, air power succeeded. If the question is asked why the bridge was struck at all, we must look not to air power but to the broader objectives and into the political decision to employ armed force.

In light of the rapid development of air power and its embodiment as the answer to all problems of surface-bound conflict, it is not surprising that distinctions have been blurred and that tactical air has been held accountable for glaring deficiencies in related but separate areas.

Amid the euphoric atmosphere associated with going in one generation from World War I surplus aircraft to jet bombers, the idea of air power's omnipotence crept in.

"We can go anywhere and do anything" became the commonly accepted opinion. If the destruction of Libyan targets says anything, it echoes that sentiment, but it does so in total disregard of all other factors influencing air power's effective use. Moreover, omnipotence has a political corollary that uses "influence" in the place of "destroy." This corollary says that by influencing A, B will be influenced and C will be influenced by B. This may be simply stated as the Billiard Effect.

The Billiard Effect avoids clear-cut objectives on which the effective use of tactical air power is based. It is as if a surgeon were asked to "influence" a ruptured appendix. With both surgery and air power, you either take it out or you do not, and it either needs to come out or it does not.

In Libya, for example, a broad objective for the use of tactical air could have been the destruction of Qaddafi's abilities to harass U.S. naval operations in the Gulf of Sidra. To assign to air power sweeping responsibilities outside the realm of destruction of targets, such as changing Qaddafi's mind about supporting terrorism or creating sufficient internal turmoil to cause his overthrow, is a fallacy.

These, or similar reasons, illustrate the greatest significance of the Billiard Effect, which is to drive the round, practical uses of air power straight into the square hole of conjecture.

The theory was tested in World War II and Korea but really came into its own during the Vietnam conflict.

In World War II, the German Blitz of London and the Allied bombing of Berlin were directed at hearts and minds. They were the wrong tools for the psychological job, and they missed the objective.

As long as weapons could be manufactured and shipped to the troops, the war continued; however, with the advent of better and faster aircraft carrying bigger payloads, the lesson of the London Blitz lay lost in the rubble.

In Vietnam, the targets, the theater of operations, and the surges and pauses were supposed to influence the behavior of the aggressor, with air power as the cue ball.

Of course, this experiment in behavior modification did not sit well with fundamentals. Intangibles, such as surprise and selective targeting of appropriate military objectives, which had the potential to render the enemy defenseless, were cast ruthlessly aside. In the end, the United States withdrew amid mumblings of, "Where did we go wrong?"

In some circles, the answer was that air power failed, disregarding the fact that the crews put the bombs on target and those targets were destroyed. Under the Billiard Effect, arrogant assumptions had pushed pragmatic application of air power out of the picture.

It became apparent that the fundamentals had been disregarded when the results of applied tactical air in the jet age did not meet expectations.

The raid on Libya clearly showed how effective improved weaponry, well-trained crews, and superb tactics could be. Hopefully, the raid on Libya also signals a turn away from the Billiard Effect and back toward realistic, specific objectives.

When national intentions are indistinct, the piecemeal use of aircraft in one brief strike should not be held culpable for what would amount to a failure to set distinct limited or broad objectives. Air power should not be held accountable for a failure of policy.

Modern tactical air power can take out a target. If that target is a bridge, the span will surely drop; if it is a building, then those that are still among the living after the walls fall down need to look for a new place to work.

What the destruction of a bridge or a building cannot do is to precisely influence how the leaders or the people of any society view the world or their relation to it.

This bleak thought in turn leads to the assessment that limited application of tactical air power is therefore useless. That is not so, but its limits must be realized. There are times when it is in the national interest to kill enemy soldiers, destroy a munitions factory, or accomplish other limited goals. Air power can do these things very effectively.

Cases in point are the Israeli strike against the Iraqi reactor or any of the strikes against Palestine Liberation Organization (PLO) camps. These were conducted in the national interest, without expectations of a dramatic victory. Although successful, the purposes were limited and the results were limited.

If you want more complete results, the broad objective must be clear and the means must match the desired outcome.

Air power is an application of force and shares that broad definition with land and sea power. The use of any of these is subject to similar limitation. For example, witness the Soviet reactions to unrest in Hungary in 1956 or in Czechoslovakia in 1968. Those rebellions were crushed because the means and tactical applications used were more than enough to accomplish the specific goal. Contrast this with Soviet actions in Afghanistan, where the goal is less distinct and the force is therefore insufficient or misapplied.

Anything short of destroying the means to wage war cannot guarantee that the war will not continue. There are no shortcuts around this elementary fact.

Evidence suggests that knowing the right targets to hit but not hitting them does not awaken the sleeping lamb of reason in a determined foe, quiet world opinion, or set the stage for letting bygones be bygones. And more to the point, it is not the purpose of air power to do any of these.

There is no doubt that air power can and does play a decisive role in warfare, yet the scope is narrow and practical. For this reason, there is a place for land, air, and sea forces--as well as politics.

To understand the basic purpose of air power is to realize that it is not omnipotent, nor is it an influence. It is, purely and simply, a means to knock down the bridge.

Chapter 5

Operation El Dorado Canyon -- The Raid on Libya

Having seen a general view of how the Reagan Administration felt about Libya, we will now look at a list of events up to and including the April 15 raid and then take a look at the world reaction to the raid.

March 10, 1981

The U.S. Sixth Fleet commenced maneuvers off shore from Libya within the Gulf of Sirte. For four days two aircraft carriers, ten other vessels and several squadrons of carrier-borne F-14 fighters conducted exercises. The Libyans, anticipating some kind of provocation, avoided reacting in haste. The intent of the Administration was to provoke an incident giving it just cause to overthrow Qaddafi.

May 6, 1981

The ordered closure of the Libyan diplomatic mission in the United States and the expulsion of all Libyan diplomatic personnel from Washington. At the same time, the State Dept. called on U.S. oil producers in

Libya (Esso, Standard, Mobil, Occidental Petroleum, Oasis Oil, Amerada Hess, Conoco, and Marathon Oil) to draw down their personnel.

June 12, 1981

The Administration announced that it would support all African nations that want to resist `interventionism' from Libya. It was reported that Tunisia, who received $15 million in military credits in 1981, would be given $95 million in FY 1982.

Sudan, which received $30 million in 1981, got $100 million in 1982. And Egypt would jump from $550 to $900 million in military credits, and from $846 for military training to $2 billion in 1982.

The Deputy Secretary of Defense told those countries in Africa neighboring Libya that "the U.S. is now willing to encourage actions against Libya although African nations would have to take the lead." The extent to which the Reagan Administration was willing to support an action against Libya was quite evident in Reagan's reported assertion to Sadat in June that the United States would back any Egyptian invasion of Libya and would take care of any attempt by the Soviets to rescue their "proxy."

July 8, 1981

The Assistant Secretary of State for African Affairs,
Chester Crocker, told Congress that the Administration
would supply arms to the African opponents of Libya 'to
help those who see the problem as we see it'. This was
still another attempt by the Administration to have
another country start a conflict with Libya and then ask
for U.S. support.

August 1981

The United States airlifted several shipments of arms to
Somalia, increased economic and military aid to the new
military regime in Liberia, and initiated a foreign
military sales and training program in Niger in an effort
to strengthen American interests in Africa.

August 19, 1981

The collision finally came in August. A giant battle
formation from the Sixth Fleet, led by the nuclear
powered aircraft carrier Nimitz, sailed into the Gulf of
Sirte to conduct further exercises specifically authorized
by the White House. The Libyans responded by sending
up two SU-22 bombers to monitor movements. Both
planes were attacked and shot down by F-14s from the
carrier Nimitz's Black Ace Squadron.

Subsequent claims that the action was preemptive are
belied by the Pentagon's own admissions that the Libyan
pilots had received no orders, transmitted by radio, to
open fire on the American planes or fleet. Had the

Libyans wanted to engage the Americans, I believe they would have been more likely to have used their MIG or Mirage fighters.

All evidence to emerge since has pointed to direct American provocation. The incident took place while Egyptian forces were conducting maneuvers at the Libyan border. Despite official U.S. claims that the Administration never intended to provoke any military confrontation with Libya, both verbal and behavioral evidence indicates that the military confrontation was planned to test Qaddafi's reactions.

Other evidence that the military provocation was preplanned was that the maneuvers were conducted below the 32-30' line, which had been drawn by the Carter Administration in talks with the Libyans as the southern most boundary for American naval and air exercises.

Reagan's response to a question about his message about the Gulf of Sirte incident also suggests its preplanned nature: "We're determined that we are going to close that window of vulnerability that has existed for some time with regard to our defensive capability."

Before the incident occurred, the Pentagon warned that the exercises would be held in a 3,200 square mile zone. The Libyans appeared to have acted when the F-14s exceeded this range. This was revealed during a press conference aboard the Nimitz on 24 Aug, when Vice Admiral Rowden admitted that the clash had occurred outside the designated area. Rear Admiral James E.

Service also said that the closest our forces came was about 25 miles off the coast whereas previously it was announced that the incident took place 60 miles out in the declared zone.

August 1981

During this period, the Reagan Administration was actively trying to secure Egyptian participation in a conflict with Libya. The American presence in the Gulf was intended to show the Egyptian President know that the U.S. would support him in an invasion of Libya. However, before the Administration's plans could become a reality, the Egyptian President was assassinated. The new Egyptian President had to take care of internal matters and again Reagan's plans for Libya had to be put on hold.

November 1981

The United States conducted a large scale military maneuver (Bright Star) on the Libyan-Egyptian border, with the participation of troops from the United States, Egypt, Sudan, Oman, and Somalia.

December 10, 1981

President Reagan asked all Americans in Libya to leave the country.

March 10, 1982

President Reagan declared an embargo on the import of crude oil from Libya and the export of U.S. technology. The pretext for this embargo was the White House claim that Libyan `hit squads' were at large in the United States on a mission to assassinate Reagan himself. No evidence was brought forward to substantiate this allegation, and the FBI has since admitted that an investigation revealed no trace of such a Libyan-backed group. The Administration called it a symbolic gesture knowing that our European allies would not follow suit. This embargo did nothing to hurt Libya, as a matter of fact it helped Europe and only hurt the American businesses.

U.S. trade with Libya in 1981-1982:

- 1981 Exports to Libya totaled 809,024

- 1982 Exports to Libya: 300,946

- 1981 Imports from Libya: 5,475,910

- 1982 Imports from Libya totaled 533,215

February 1983

The prospects of military confrontation rose again when Reagan reacted to a claim by President Numeiri to have unearthed a Libyan conspiracy with a massive show of strength directed against Libya.

The speed of the military build-up was surprising and gave the impression that an actual invasion might be imminent. It looked like the U.S. was going to finish what it had started the year before when they backed off almost as suddenly as it began. The de-escalation stemmed from the Egyptian government's reluctance to become embroiled on the United States behalf. Reagan had reacted quickly and thought he could claim he was supporting Egypt while destroying Qaddafi, but once again he had to pull back.

One senior Egyptian official quoted in the Times' on 21 February fulminated angrily, "We are furious.   The Americans are trying to implicate us in things that do not involve us." Numeiri never did furnish any proof that there was a Libyan threat against his regime.

August 1983

Almost an exact replay of what occurred in February occurred again. This time it was an accusation by Hissene Habre that Libya had invaded Chad. Once again a military force was sent to the Gulf with Reagan hoping for Egyptian involvement, and once again Egypt refused.

March 1984

Sudan claimed that Libya bombed the Omdurman radio station. For once, the Egyptians somewhat relented and, under their 1975 defense pact with Sudan, dispatched troops to reinforce Numeiri's forces. But Egypt's president was only willing to reinforce defenses and no more. He was not interested in a conflict with Libya.

November 3, 1985

The Washington Post discloses that two months earlier President Reagan had formally approved a CIA plan for a Coup d'etat in Libya.

November 15, 1985

Executive order 12538: Imports of Refined Petroleum Products From Libya. An order from Reagan banning the import of all Petroleum products from Libya by the U.S., its territories or possessions.

January 7, 1986

Executive order 12543: Prohibiting Trade And Certain Transactions Involving Libya. President Reagan considered Libya a threat to U.S.

interests and declares a national emergency,
further limiting transactions with Libya. In a
Statement to the press that same day, Reagan
says, "Qaddafi deserves to be treated as a pariah
in the world community.

January 8, 1986

Executive order 12544:   Blocking Libyan
government Property In The United States or
Held By U.S. persons. Reagan blocked all
property or interests in properties of Libya.

March 14, 1986

U.S. navy vessels again sailed into the Gulf of
Sidra near the radar stations of Sirte, challenging
Qaddafi to respond, and this time he did. By the
time the confrontation ended on March 17, the
United States reported sinking two Libyan
vessels and temporarily shutting down an SA-5
missile base. U.S. officials hailed the operation
as a victory and claimed that it diminished the
Soviets' prestige both by revealing the inferiority
of the weapons supplied by the Soviet Union to
Libya and by exposing their reluctance to do
anything other than light up their ships and head
for safety when fighting broke out.

For his part, Reagan proclaimed the operation "a message to the whole world that the United States has the will and the ability to defend the free world's interests."

April 15, 1986

At 2am Libyan time, aircraft from the United States' Airforce and Navy struck at six main targets in the vicinity of Tripoli and Benghazi. According to U.S. official figures, a total of 36 people were killed; journalists in the Libyan capital, however, estimated that there were over 100 dead and twice that many wounded. Among the known casualties were members of Qaddafi's own family; his wife Safia, and three of the couple's children suffered pressure shock from the blast of a 2,000 lb. bomb. Hours later Qaddafi's sixteen month-old adopted daughter Hanna died from brain damage. Qaddafi who had taken the precaution to sleep in an underground office, was not injured.

The U.S. attack was set in motion when F-111 bombers, radar jamming planes and refueling planes took off from four bases in Great Britain. The planes detoured around Spain, adding 2,400 miles to the round trip. France refused to allow the planes to fly over its territory. In the Mediterranean north of Libya, A-6E Navy bombers left the carriers America and Coral Sea at around 1:00 am Libyan time. The main attacks began about an hour later, with 13 F-111s striking targets in and around Tripoli and a dozen A-6Es attacking two sites in the northeastern part of Libya.

Working with carrier aircraft of the U.S. Sixth Fleet, Air Force F-111s of the 48th Tactical Fighter Wing flew what turned out to be the longest fighter combat mission in history. The crushing strikes reportedly caused a remarkable reduction in Libyan sponsored terrorist activity.

In the mid-1980s, the F-111s of the 48th TFW, stationed at RAF Lakenheath in Britain, formed a key element of NATO power. If war came, the Aardvark's long range and night, low-level bombing capability would have been vital in defeating a Soviet attack. To the south, in the Mediterranean, the Sixth Fleet engaged Soviet warships in a constant game of mutual surveillance and stayed in more or less permanent readiness for hostilities.

Fate would dictate that the 48th TFW and Sixth Fleet carriers would be teamed in a totally unexpected quarter against a very different kind of enemy. They would strike not in or around Europe but on the North African littoral. They would go into action not against Soviet conventional forces but against an Arab state bent on sponsoring deadly terrorist acts.

The Sixth Fleet, based in the Mediterranean Sea, began a series of maneuvers designed to keep pressure on Libya. Two, and sometimes three, aircraft carriers (namely, Saratoga, America, and Coral Sea) conducted "freedom of navigation" operations that would take U.S. warships up to and then southward across a line at 32 degrees 30 minutes north latitude. This was Qaddafi's self-proclaimed "Line of Death."

The Line of Death defined the northernmost edge of the Gulf of Sidra and demarcated it--in Qaddafi's mind, at least--from the rest of the Mediterranean. The Libyan leader had warned foreign vessels that the Gulf belonged to Libya and was not international waters. The message was that they entered at their own risk and were subject to attack by Libyan forces.

Thus, Qaddafi, by drawing the Line, unilaterally sought to exclude U.S. ships and aircraft from a vast, 3,200-square-mile area of the Med., which had always been considered international.

The skirmishing soon began. On March 24, 1986, Libyan air defense operators fired SA-5 missiles at two F-14s. The Tomcats had intercepted an intruding MiG-25 that came a bit too close to a battle group.

The next day, a Navy A-7E aircraft struck the SAM site with AGM-88A HARM missiles. At least two of the five threatening Libyan naval attack vessels were also sunk.

In the months leading up to the Berlin bombing, planners at USAF's 48th TFW had developed more than 30 plans for delivering a punitive blow against Libya. Most were variations on a theme--six or so Air Force F-111 fighter-bombers would fly through French airspace and strike selected military targets in Libya.

Planners assumed that the attack would have the benefit of surprise; the small number of F-111s made it probable that the bombers would be in and out before the Libyan defenses were alerted.

Later, when detailed speculation in the Western media lessened the probability of surprise, attack plans were changed to include support packages that would carry out suppression of enemy air defenses. These packages were to comprise Air Force EF-111 electronic warfare aircraft as well as Navy A-7 and EA-6B aircraft. This was the start of an Air Force-Navy liaison that would prove essential in the actual mission.

However, all the 48th's plans had been rendered obsolete by April 1986. Continuous media coverage, apparently fueled by leaks from very senior and knowledgeable sources in the White House, had rendered surprise almost impossible.

Moreover, the U.S. was having serious trouble with its Allies. Britain's Prime Minister, Margaret Thatcher, approved U.S. use of British bases to launch the attack. However, Washington's other Allies lost their nerve. The fear of reprisals and loss of business caused France, Germany, Italy, and Spain to refuse to cooperate in a strike.

The faintheartedness of these countries forced the U.S. to prepare a radically different attack plan. USAF F-111s would now navigate around France and Spain, thread the needle through the airspace over the narrow Strait of Gibraltar, and then plunge on eastward over the Mediterranean until in a position to attack.

It would prove to be a grueling round-trip flight of 6,400 miles that spanned 13 hours, requiring eight to 12 in-flight refuelings for each aircraft. Inasmuch as a standard NATO F-111 sortie was about two hours, the El Dorado Canyon mission placed a tremendous strain on crews and complex avionic systems at the heart of the aircraft.

U.S. authorities crafted a joint operation of the Air Force and Navy against five major Libyan targets. Of these, two were in Benghazi: a terrorist training camp and the military airfield. The other three were in Tripoli:

1) a terrorist naval training base;

2) the former Wheelus AFB; and

3) the Azziziyah Barracks compound, which housed the command center for Libyan intelligence and contained one of five residences that Qaddafi used.

Eighteen F-111s were assigned to strike the three Tripoli targets, while Navy aircraft were to hit the two Benghazi sites. Navy aircraft also were to provide air defense suppression for both phases of the operation. U.S. authorities gave overall command to Vice Admiral Frank B. Kelso II, Commander of the Sixth Fleet.

The composition of the El Dorado Canyon force has stirred controversy. In his 1988 book, *Command of the Seas*, former Navy Secretary John F. Lehman Jr. said the entire raid could have been executed by aircraft from Air Craft Carriers America and Coral Sea.

This claim cropped up again in 1997 in a letter to Foreign Affairs, Marine Major General John H. Admire, an operations planner in U.S. European Command at the time. The letter said, "Sufficient naval forces were available to execute the attacks." Both attributed USAF's participation to a bureaucratic need to placate the Air Force.

The fact of the matter, however, is the Air Force had long been preparing for such a raid. When Washington decreed that there would be only one attack, it became absolutely necessary to mount a joint operation because only the inclusion of heavy USAF attack aircraft could provide the firepower needed to ensure that the operation would be more than a pinprick attack.

The Navy had only America and Coral Sea on station. According to Air Force officials involved in the plans, these two carriers did not have sufficient aircraft for effective attacks against all five targets in both Tripoli and Benghazi. At least one more carrier, and perhaps two, would have been required, said these officers.

The act of calling in a third or even a fourth carrier to handle both targets would have caused a delay and given away any remaining element of surprise.

This fact was pointed out to the Chairman of the Joint Chiefs of Staff, Admiral William J. Crowe Jr. Crowe himself recognized that F-111s were needed if both Tripoli and Benghazi were to be struck at more or less the same time. They would also add an element of surprise and a new axis of attack.

For these reasons, the JCS Chairman recommended to Reagan and the National Security Council that the United States use both Air Force and Navy aircraft in the raids.

The F-111Fs of the 48th were special birds, equipped with two Pratt & Whitney TF-30 P-100 turbofan engines of 25,100 pounds of thrust each and a highly classified AN/AVQ-26 Pave Tack bombing system. Pave Tack consisted of an infrared camera and laser designator. It enabled the F-111 crew to see the target in the dark or through light fog or dust obscurations (not heavy dust and smoke).

When the target was seen, it was designated by the energy of a laser beam. The 2,000-pound GBU-10 Paveway II laser-guided bomb tracked the laser to the illuminated target. Pave Tack imparted to the F-111s a limited standoff capability, achieved by lobbing the bombs at the target. As events unfolded, the Pave Tack equipment would be crucial to the mission's success.

On April 14, at 17:36 Greenwich Mean Time, 24 Aardvarks departed Lakenheath with the intent that six would return after the first refueling about 90 minutes out. Also launched were five EF-111 electronic warfare aircraft. This marked the start of the first U.S. bomber attack from the United Kingdom since World War II.

The tanker force was launched at roughly the same time as the F-111s, four of which joined up on their respective "mother tankers" in radio silence, flying such a tight formation that radar controllers would see only the tanker signatures on their screens.

At the first refueling, six F-111Fs and one EF-111A broke off and returned to base. Beyond Lands End, UK, the aircraft would be beyond the control of any international authority, operating at 26,000 feet and speeds up to 450 knots.

To save time and ease navigation, tankers were to accompany the fighters to and from the target area. KC-10 tankers, called in from Barksdale Air Force Base, LA., March AFB, CA., and Seymour Johnson AFB, N.C., were refueled in turn by KC-135s, assigned to the 300th Strategic Wing, RAF Mildenhall, and the 11th Strategic Group, RAF Fairford, UK.

What had been drafted as a small, top secret mission had changed drastically. The force now included 18 USAF strike aircraft and four EF-111F electronic warfare aircraft from the 42d Electronic Combat Squadron, RAF Upper Heyford, UK. The lead KC-10 controlled the F-111s.

The size of the attack force went against the judgment of the 48th's leadership, including that of its commander, Colonel Sam W. Westbrook III. With the possibility of surprise gone, the 48th felt that the extra aircraft meant there would be too much time over target, particularly for the nine aircraft assigned to strike the Azziziyah Barracks. Libyan defenses, already on alert, would have time to concentrate on the later waves of attackers.

Secretary of Defense Casper Weinberger, however, was an advocate of a larger strike, and he was supported in this by Gen. Charles A. Gabriel, Chief of Staff of the Air Force, Gen. Charles L. Donnelly Jr., Commander of United States Air Forces in Europe, and Maj. Gen. David W. Forgan, Donnelly's operations deputy. The three USAF officers believed the large force increased the possibility of doing substantial damage to the targets.

On the Navy side, the Sixth Fleet was to attack with the forces arrayed on two carriers. Coral Sea launched eight A-6E medium bombers for the attack and six F/A-18C Hornets for strike support. America launched six A-6Es for the attack and six A-7Es and an EA-6B for strike support. F-14s protected the fleet and aircraft.

A high alert status characterized Soviet vessels in the Mediterranean monitoring ship and aircraft movement. Libya's vast air defense system was sophisticated, and its operators were acutely aware that an attack was coming.

In the wake of the raid, the U.S. compared the Libyan network with target complexes in the Soviet Union and its satellites. Only three were found to have had stronger defenses than the Libyan cities.

The difficulties of the mission were great. Most of the crews had never seen combat. Most had never refueled from a KC-10, and none had done so at night in radio silence. The strike force did benefit from the presence of highly experienced flight leaders, many of them Vietnam combat veterans. They were flying the longest and most demanding combat mission in history against alerted defenses--and doing it in coordination with a naval force more than 3,000 miles distant.

Timing was absolutely critical, and the long route and multiple refuelings increased the danger of a disastrous error. The Air Force and Navy attacks had to be simultaneous to maximize any remaining element of surprise and to get strike aircraft in and out as quickly as possible.

Mission difficulty was compounded by rigorous Rules of Engagement. These ROE stipulated that, before an attack could go forward, the target had to be identified through multiple sources and all mission-critical F-111 systems had to be operating well. Any critical system failure required an immediate abort, even if an F-111 was in the last seconds of its bomb run.

At about midnight GMT, six flights of three F-111Fs each bore down on Tripoli. Fatigue of the long mission was forgotten as the pilots monitored their terrain-following equipment. The weapon system officers prepared for the attack, checking the navigation, looking for targets and offset aiming points, and, most important of all, checking equipment status.

The first three attacking elements, code-named Remit, Elton, and Karma, were tasked to hit Qaddafi's headquarters at the Azziziyah Barracks. This target included a command and control center, but not the Libyan leader's nearby residence and the Bedouin-style tent he often used.

Westbrook proved to be prescient in his belief that nine aircraft were too many to be put against the Azziziyah Barracks, as only two of the nine aircraft dropped their bombs. These, however, would prove to be tremendously important strikes.

- One element, "Jewel," struck the Sidi Balal terrorist training camp where there was a main complex, a secondary academy, a Palestinian training camp, and a maritime academy under construction. Jewel's attack was successful, taking out the area where naval commandos trained.

- Two elements, "Puffy" and "Lujac," were armed with Mk 82 Snakeeye parachute-retarded 500-pound bombs, and they struck the Tripoli airport, destroying three Ilyushin IL-76 transports and damaging three others as well as destroying a Boeing 727 and a Fiat G 222.

Flying in support of the F-111 attacks were EF-111As and Navy A-7s, A-6Es, and an EA-6B, using HARM and Shrike anti-radar missiles.

Similar defense suppression support, including F/A-18s, was provided across the Gulf of Sidra, where Navy A-6E aircraft were to attack the Al Jumahiriya Barracks at Benghazi, and the Benina airfield to the east. The Navy's Intruders destroyed four MiG-23s, two Fokker F-27s, and two Mil Mi-8 helicopters.

The Air Force F-111Fs would spend only 11 minutes in the target area, with what at first appeared to be mixed results. Anti-aircraft and SAM opposition from the very first confirmed that the Libyans were ready.

News of the raid was broadcast while it was in progress.

One aircraft, Karma 52, was lost, almost certainly due to a SAM, as it was reported to be on fire in flight. Capt. Fernando L. Ribas-Dominicci and Capt. Paul F. Lorence were killed. Only Ribas-Dominicci's body was recovered; his remains were returned to the U.S. three years later.

As each F-111 aircraft exited the target area, they gave a coded transmission, with "Tranquil Tiger" indicating success and "Frostee Freezer" indicating that the target was not hit. Then the crews, flushed with adrenaline from the attack, faced a long flight home, with more in-flight refuelings, the knowledge that one aircraft was down, and the incredible realization that the raid's results were already being broadcast on Armed Forces Radio. The news included comments from Weinberger and Secretary of State George P. Shultz. One F-111F had to divert to Rota Air Base, Spain, because of an engine overheat. The mission crew was returned to Lakenheath within two hours.

Early and fragmentary USAF post strike analysis raised some questions about the performance of the F-111s. Even though all three targets had been successfully struck, only four of the 18 F-111s dropped successfully. Six were forced to abort due to aircraft difficulties or stringencies of the Rules of Engagement. Seven missed their targets and one was lost. There had been collateral damage, with one bomb landing near the French Embassy.

The combined Air Force-Navy raid resulted in 130 civilian casualties with 37 killed, including, it was claimed, the adopted daughter of Qaddafi.

Yet events were soon to prove that the raid had been a genuine success, and as time passed, its beneficial effects would be recognized. It quickly became obvious that Qaddafi, who had exultantly backed the bombing of others, was terribly shaken when the bombs fell near him.

His house had been damaged and flying debris had reportedly injured his shoulder. He disappeared from the scene for 24 hours, inspiring some speculation that he had been killed. When he did reappear on a television broadcast, he was obviously deeply disturbed, lacking his usual arrogance.

Libya protested but received only muted support from Arab nations. In its comments, Moscow was curiously nonjudgmental and withheld a strong endorsement of Qaddafi. More importantly, the following months would see a dramatic decrease in the number of Libyan-sponsored, anti-American terrorist events.

The Red Army Faction, one of the groups that had claimed responsibility for the La Belle disco bombing, reduced its activities. Other Libyan-sponsored groups followed suit.

White House officials said the targets of the raid were only terrorist installations and infrastructure. Contrary to the impression given by American spokesmen, not to mention the president himself, the weight of the evidence indicates a powerful military assault on the apparatus of the Libyan state.

The targets of the operation did not correspond with the qualification "terrorist installation" or "infrastructure," all were key points in Qaddafi's system of command and control. They were Qaddafi's headquarters and command center at Bab al-Azizya; his alternative command post, and the base of the Islamic Legion, at the Jamahiriya Barracks outside Benghazi; the headquarters of the Security Service in central Tripoli; Sidi Bilal naval base and academy to the east of Tripoli; and the country's two main airports, Tripoli and Benina, near Benghazi. In addition there was a series of supplementary strikes against signal and radar installations.

There is evidence that Qaddafi was a target, which makes it an assassination attempt. This is, of course, denied by Reagan and his officials. *The Washington Post* quoted unnamed Administration officials on April 18 as saying that the bombing of Bab al-Azizya Barracks, in the first wave of a two-wave attack, was intended to kill Qaddafi.

Even before the Administration had received knowledge of Qaddafi's fate, officials of the National Security Council had drafted a statement describing his death as "fortuitous."

Despite the failure to locate Qaddafi, his downfall remained the principal objective of the U.S. action. The bombings were meant to either kill Qaddafi or produce tensions within the Libyan armed forces, prompting discontented officers into an attempted coup.

Because of CIA reports during the months before the raid, the Reagan Administration firmly believed that if the bombs missed Qaddafi then his military would overthrow him anyway. Once again, Reagan came out frustrated in not being able to topple the Libyan leader.

This data shows that between March 10, 1981 and the April 15, 1986 raid, there were numerous attempts politically, economically, and militarily by the United States to provoke a confrontation with Libya. During this time, terrorism was never given as a reason for U.S. actions until the raid itself.

The bombing of Libya was said to be in response to Libyan terrorism, but the United States was never able to produce clear evidence of such activity.

The first reason for the bombing was stated in advance of the attack. According to the *New York Times*, April 3, 1986, Secretary of State George Shultz (later an adviser to George W. Bush as he campaigned in

2000 for the presidency) said on March 28, that Washington had long wanted to "blow the whistle" on Colonel Moamar Qaddafi because he "is doing things that are against our interests."

Reagan's subsequent action was an act of aggression—or undeclared war. He didn't consult Congress, as required by law, or the United Nations, as required by its charter.

The facts as presented show the possibility that the term terrorism was used by the Administration as a key issue to justify a military raid on Libya, only after years of trying to overtly and covertly overthrow the Qaddafi regime had not worked.

Another way of looking at this possibility is to see if other nations supported the U.S. action. If they didn't, then that might indicate that they may have considered the raid as more than just a strike against terrorism, possibly even as just one more step in the American anti-Libya foreign policy.

If the downfall of this dangerous "Mad Dog" Qaddafi was for the good of the world, then the other nations should have been behind the U.S. on this attack. Shouldn't they?

If this raid were a response toward terrorism as the Reagan Administration proclaimed, then wouldn't it be logical to assume that the other major powers would be happy for the American help?

Of course, if the reason for the raid was not a response to stop terrorism, then our allies might not think the way the Reagan Administration thought. Among the European Community's 12-member governments, 11 of them NATO allies of the United States, Britain was the only one to initially voice support. The only nations that could be construed to have supported the American action were Britain, Canada, and Israel.

World reaction to the raid, especially in the Arab, African and Islamic worlds, was generally hostile. The Non-Aligned Movement condemned the attack as a blatant, unprovoked act of aggression; and as a demonstration of support, it sent a delegation to Libya on 20 April. The OPEC member states also condemned the attack but rejected a Libyan demand for an immediate oil embargo against the United States.

Moderate Arab states, such as Egypt and Jordan, were trapped between traditional ties of Arab solidarity and uneasiness over American actions.

The lack of support, and even opposition, suggest that strategic factors were of primary importance in the U.S. image of and policy toward Libya. This is true despite the official U.S. claim that the reason for the United States hostility is Libya's support of terrorism.

In other words, the perception of Libya as a proxy of the Soviet Union is the most important variable in understanding U.S. policy.

Reagan's actions brought strong reaction and comments by many of the major states:

Great Britain:

Margaret Thatcher supported the U.S. action even though polls showed that a majority of Britain did not. Even Thatcher was hesitant and did not appear to be totally for it, but after Reagan's help in the Falkland

Islands, she owed a big favor and really could not turn her back on Reagan's request. Reagan needed Britain for political reasons not military ones. There were plenty of military capabilities in the Gulf off shore from Libya to accomplish Reagan's intent without the use of American bases in Britain. Margaret Thatcher drew criticism and lost popularity among voters, while Reagan gained popularity among Americans.

West Germany:

While Helmut Kohl and West Germany opposed the raid, they at least expressed a feeling of understanding for Reagan's reasons even though they felt it would not accomplish anything.

The German Foreign Minister Hans-Dietrich Gunscher, justified his government's refusal to go along with the U.S. policy on Libya by saying that "the U.S. was wrong in trying to isolate Libya or depict the Libyan leader as a Soviet pawn."

Italy:

Italy opposed the raid and thought America was going to cause more world problems with actions that they didn't understand.

Prime Minister Bettino Craxi said, "Far from weakening terrorism, this military action risks provoking explosive reactions of fanaticism and criminal and suicide acts."

France:

France refused to allow American aircraft to fly over their airspace, and after the raid announced that they deplored the American action.

Greece:

Greece was probably the most outspoken and blunt European opponent of the raid, and demanded an immediate EEC (European Economic Community) meeting. Mr. Andreas Pompandreou said, "The raid was violence in the face of violence, but it sets dynamite to peace and destroys the independence of a nation in the name of imposing a hegemonistic United States presence in the area."

Belgium:

The Belgium leader Mr. Leo Tindemans sums up his country's feelings in one statement, "We regret that the Americans used military action. We do not think the sixth fleet is the best way to fight terrorism."

Spain:

Spain also refused to allow the U.S. to use its airspace and disapproved of the raid. Prime Minister Filipe Gonzalez said, "I do not agree with the method used."

Chapter 6

Relevant International Law

A. *The Use of Force*

The Pacific settlement of disputes is a fundamental principle of the international legal system and is enshrined in Articles 2(3) and 33 of the United Nations Charter, which provides that states finding themselves in dispute should, in the first instance, attempt to reach a mutually satisfactory settlement and, failing this, refer the question to the Security Council. Article 2(4) of the Charter places restrictions on the use of force. It provides:

> All members shall refrain in their international relations from the use or threat or use of force against the territorial integrity of political independence of any state, or any other manner inconsistent with the purposes of the United Nations.

There are, however, some exceptions to the prohibition on the use of force. These have been categorized as follows:

1. acts of self-defense;

2. acts of collective self-defense;

3. actions authorized by a competent international organ;

4. situations where treaties confer rights to intervene by an ad hoc invitation, or where consent is given by the territorial sovereign;

5. actions to terminate trespass;

6. necessity arising from natural catastrophe; and

7. measures to protect the lives and or property of nationals in a foreign territory.

Factors to consider in analyzing a self-help measure are:

1) whether the action takes on a remedial or repressive character to enforce legal rights,

2) whether the force applied supports the notions of basic community order, and

3) whether the force has been applied in ways whose consequences conform to community goals and minimal world order.

B. *The Protection of Nationals Abroad*

The right to use force to protect nationals abroad is well recognized in international law. Any national government will maintain concern for the safety of its nationals abroad; it has been postulated that an injury to a national in a foreign state is an imputed injury to the national's home state. The American and Israeli governments have frequently called upon this concept to justify their intervention in other countries.

The following conditions must be satisfied in order for a nation to legally use force:

1. an imminent threat of injury to nationals must exist;

2. the territorial sovereign must fail or be unable to protect them; and

3. the measure of protection must be strictly confined to the object of protecting the nationals against injury.

Such use of force must always be on a limited, temporary and proportionate basis. The use of any more force than strictly necessary to protect nationals is a violation of the United Nations Charter.

C. *Anticipatory Self-defense*

Article 51 of the United Nations Charter provides:

> Nothing in the present Charter shall impair the inherent right of individual or collective self-defense if an armed attack occurs against a Member of the United Nations, until the Security Council has taken measures to maintain international peace and security. Measures taken by members in the exercise of this right of self-defense shall be immediately reported to the Security Council and shall not in any way affect the authority and responsibility of the Security Council under the present Charter to take at any time such action as it deems necessary in order to maintain or restore international peace and security.

There is some debate as to whether this article permits pre-emptive strikes in anticipatory self-defense. Concern over the possible abuse of such an exemption to Article 51 has prompted scholars such as legal Professors Henkin, Jessup, Brownlie and Kunz to contend that to allow such an exception would allow a nation to launch pre-emptive attacks.

On the other side of the coin, noted legal scholars such as Professor Bowett, McDougal and Waldcock have acknowledged the validity of the concept of anticipatory self-defense pending certain requirements. Recently, nations such as the United States and Israel have advocated the desirability of the doctrine, especially in the area of responding to terrorists.

Indeed, these nations have applied this principle in practice: Israel against the PLO (in, for example, the air strike against Tunis, on October 2, 1985); and the U.S. against Libya (in the incident being considered), and in the invasion of Grenada.

The use of such self-defense is a temporary remedy only and the right to use force ends once the United Nations (through the Security Council) itself takes action. It is important to note also that reprisals are illegal in international law. Professor Bowett has stated that

> [s]elf-defense is permissible for the purpose of protecting the security of the state and the essential rights in particular the rights of territorial integrity and political independence upon which that security depends. In contrast, reprisals are punitive in character; they seek to impose reparation for the harm done, or to compel a satisfactory settlement of the dispute created by the initial illegal act, or to compel the delinquent state to abide by the law in future.

Bowett has, however, also noted that some reprisals will avoid condemnation and such acts will gradually become *de facto* (if not *de jure*) legal.

If states can indeed legally use force as a pre-emptive measure against the threat of terrorist attack, if not as a reprisal, what factors need to be considered in a justification of such action?   There are two main considerations here:

> first, necessity (of a temporal nature, *i.e.* responding close in time to the impending threat) and

> second, a requirement of proportionality of response.

The *locus classicus* on anticipatory self-defense is *The Caroline*. During a rebellion in colonial Canada in 1837, a boat crewed by American volunteers, at the time on the American side of the Niagara River, was stormed by British forces.

According to Professor Oscar Schachter:

> Secretary Webster [the then U.S. Secretary of State] denied the necessity of self-defense in those circumstances, asserting ... that self-defense must be confined to cases in which the necessity of that self-defense is instant, overwhelming, and leaving no choice of means, and no moment for deliberation.

Professor Schachter also states that in the Security Council debates on the Israeli air strike on the Osirak nuclear reactor in Iraq, reference was made by delegates to the *Caroline* case, from which can be inferred that the UN may recognize a continuing right to the use of pre-emptive strikes in self-defense, but only where attack is imminent.

The doctrine has been called upon as a defense for the Japanese invasion of Manchuria in 1933, for the Nazi invasion of Norway in 1940 (in both cases, this was rejected by international tribunals) and for the American blockade of Cuba in 1962.

In more recent times, the Israeli government used it as justification for its air strike against the Iraqi nuclear reactor at Osirak in 1981, for its invasion of Lebanon and for its bombing of the PLO Headquarters in Tunis in 1985. These latter cases have never been judicially considered. The standard advanced by legal scholars is that the nation should act with "reasonableness under the circumstances".

According to Professor Schachter, "defensive retaliation" may be allowable if there is reason to expect attacks which would be prevented by such retaliation, but the use of force to exact revenge or impose a penalty would be illegal in international law.

In summary, states may not use force as an instrument of revenge or as a tool of vindication, but may use it as a response to attack, provided such use is necessary and proportionate.

D. *The Extra-Territorial Use of Force against Terrorists*

In relation to the specific question of the extra-territorial use of force against terrorist bases, a set of questions should be considered:

1. *Does Article 51 or relevant customary law allow extraterritorial use of force in response to an armed attack by a non-state group?*

   It would not.

2. *Is an attack by terrorists on nationals of a particular state outside of that state an armed attack on the state?*

"[W]hen such attacks are aimed at the government or intended to change a policy of that state, the attacks are reasonably considered as attacks on the state in question.

3. *Is an attack on persons within a state that is not itself the political target of the terrorists an attack on the territorial state?*

As this violates that states territorial integrity, it as an attack justifying self-defense.

4. *Would evidence of a terrorist base in a foreign country and of preparations to attack the target state legally justify an armed pre-emptive attack by the latter?*

It would not, unless the threatened attack was imminent and armed self-defense required a pre-emptive strike as a matter of necessity.

5. *Where a terrorist attack on a citizen or instrumentality of the target state has occurred, would that state have a right to attack terrorists in another country as a reprisal or punitive action?*

As we have seen, "punitive reprisals are legally forbidden."

6. *Does the state that suffered a terrorist attack have to prove that its counter-attack on the terrorist base is "necessary"?*

This requirement of necessity remains a condition of self-defense under the Charter as under customary law.

7. *Are there appropriate legal criteria for determining the necessity for self-defense?*

Identified factors are: the pattern of prior attacks, the ignoring of warnings, the attempt to use peaceful means and complicity or responsibility of the state in which the bases are located.

8. *Is the requirement of proportionality meaningful?*

This is held to be very important, either in comparison to the single attack that preceded the retaliation, in relation to a continuing pattern of attacks or in terms of the end sought and the means used.

What level of attack gives rise to a right of response? The academic debate presents us with varied opinions. The right to self-defense itself is unquestioned. Marking the point on the continuum where terrorist attacks legitimize the use of force is a point of contention.

Some legal minds favor a high threshold and believe that states may respond only to terrorist attacks *within their own territory*. Others would set the threshold much lower. There are also those in the middle ground, preferring a moderate threshold, who believe that single terrorist attacks would not justify the use of force, but that *large-scale, continuing attacks* might do so.

An analysis of state practice since the Second World War holds three conclusions:

1) that only the United States and Israel have used force in response to terrorism;

2) that these actions have been few and geographically limited to the Middle East; and

3) that the Security Council has fairly routinely condemned Israeli and American forcible actions.

Contemporary legal scholarship has remained bitterly divided over the question of forcible state responses to terrorism and at least two contrasting versions of authoritative state practice can be advanced: firstly, that a state only has a right to take forcible action after a terrorist attack in its territory; or alternatively, taking into account the interests of states whose interests have been specially affected by terrorism, that counter-terror reprisals are not prohibited.

There is a fundamental problem in considering the international law with regard to the use of force in general: there is no final judicial arbiter in such matters, and the statements of all the participants are politically loaded and cannot be regarded as legally accurate.

An examination of the UN Security Council debates on the U.S. raid on Libya, and the use made of them by scholars, will develop this point and provide us with a proper perspective before moving on to consider the question of proof of Libyan complicity in the original terrorist act. The security council debate can be summarized as follows:

> In a series of eight meetings, the Security Council considered the raid on Libya. Here, the American recourse to force was criticized on a variety of bases and by representatives from numerous states including Algeria, Cuba, Czechoslovakia, East Germany, Ghana, India, Oman, Saudi Arabia, the Soviet Union, Syria, the United Arab Emirates, and Qatar.

Council delegates maintained that the use of armed force against Libya had been, *inter alia*, "indiscriminate," pursuant to no prior "armed attack," pursuant to no substantiated Libyan involvement in "terrorist" activities; part of a broader pattern of American aggression against "progressive" Third World states; designed to thwart Libya's support of "wars of national liberation;" and exemplary of "state terrorism."

A draft resolution condemning the American action was defeated due to American exercise of its veto power--Bulgaria, China, the Congo, Ghana, Madagascar, Thailand, Trinidad and Tobago, the USSR and the United Arab Emirates voted in favor. Australia, Denmark, France, the UK and the USA voted against, and Venezuela abstained. The General Assembly, however, adopted a condemnatory resolution by a vote of 79-28-33 (for-against-abstentions).

In the literature, scholars tend to rely more on each other than on the pronouncements of states in the United Nations as a means of establishing the international law, although it is clear the writers have read the records of the relevant debates. This may be because the legal grounds asserted by states in such forum are inherently suspect as being legal rationalizations for a political decision. The UN forum is therefore rarely even quasi-judicial in nature and are at heart political institutions, especially the Security Council. Indeed, it could be said that the international legal system breaks down when it comes to the use of force:

> ... every time a government uses force or responds to such use by others, it invokes the law along with considerations of morality and humanity. This very fact generates cynicism since it seems possible for every action to find support in law and there appears no effective higher authority to settle the matter. These facts understandably lead many to conclude that the

legal rules on the use of force may be used to rationalize and justify almost any use of force and, therefore, that they can have little if any influence on the actual decision to use force.

Such eminent scholars as Professor Oscar Schachter have acknowledged that the lack of an authoritative body to decide conflicts makes international law no more than paper rules. Schachter himself rejects this criticism, but it is interesting to note on this point that, in 1993, on the occasion of the American attack in retaliation for an alleged Iraqi plot to murder former President George Bush, detailed evidence of the plan was presented to the Security Council. No such information was put forward with regard to the alleged Libyan complicity in the Berlin disco bomb, apparently because of the need to protect the sources of the information. It is likely that world reaction to such actions are formed at least as much by political as by legal concerns.

One of the fundamental problems of the international legal system is the Security Council veto; this allows the permanent members (the United States, Russia (formerly the Soviet Union), France, the United Kingdom and China) to prevent the passing of any resolutions of which they disapprove.

While this does not allow them to force the Council to adopt resolutions, it ensures that it is rare that the Council can censure a permanent member; this runs counter to the fundamental legal principle of *nemo iudex in sua causa* (meaning, the decision maker must be impartial; the deciding authority must be free from bias and prejudice; and more literally, no one should be able to make decisions concerning his own cause).

Given this, and the nature of the debates, which are often convened quickly and are attended by career diplomats rather than trained lawyers, the decisions of UN bodies are not to be regarded as always definitive and are not legally binding unless part of a mandatory decision of the Security Council.

This lack of legal rigor in one of the most important international forums to consider the use of force considerably weakens the strength of the prohibition contained in the United Nations Charter, and allows states (especially permanent members of the Security Council) to flout the provisions of this fundamental document at their convenience.

In the case of the debate on the Libyan bombing, few states presented coherent legal analysis of the facts. Those that did (for example the Ambassador from the then German Democratic Republic), even when they seem legally rigorous, are so obviously politically motivated as to have little persuasive or objective value. Some of the contributions of the delegates are worthy of note, however.

The Qatari Ambassador, Mr. Al-Kawari, gives a lengthy and detailed overview of the relevant international law, concluding that "[t]he only possible description of the operation is aggression according to Article 2(4) of the Charter." The Algerian delegation raised the interesting point that as the Security Council was aware of the situation in the Gulf of Sidra, the United States was under a duty not to hinder possible future United Nations efforts. This sentiment was echoed by the Ambassador for Madagascar.

For the most part, however, the legal content of most of the debate is low, with the United States and its allies invoking their right of self-defense and listing past Libyan outrages, while the Libyan Ambassador, Mr. Treiki, claimed that "[t]he United States is acting according to the law of the jungle."

Some of those present at the Security Council noted this problem:

> ...I find that in this debate it is as if we were living in two worlds. We are still in the habit of talking at each other instead of to each other.

Was the American action legal under international law? The academic writings on the question provide us with differing viewpoints. We should turn to the previously mentioned eight questions as a useful guide and arrive at our own conclusion. The force used was directed against the Libyan state; therefore, it would generally be prohibited as an unlawful use of force under Article 2(4) of the Charter.

As the bombing of the Berlin disco would seem to have been an implicit targeting of the American servicemen who frequented it, there was, however, an attack on the American state from which it was entitled to defend itself. The violation of the territorial integrity of Germany (which undoubtedly occurred) is irrelevant to our discussion, as it was never raised in argument by any party to the debate.

The next questions provide more food for thought: was there really evidence to conclusively link the Libyan government to imminent attacks on American targets? Or was the American action really just a punitive strike at Qaddafi by an administration frustrated at his intransigence, especially coming so soon after the "border incident" in the Gulf of Sidra? Was it really necessary to use air strikes against the Libyan government? Was the American response proportional?

Let's consider these questions in inverse order.

Proportionality has been defined as "an attack on a military objective is unlawful if it causes damage to the civilian population out of all proportion to the military advantage gained." That the civilian population should be protected from the use of force by governments is clear.

In this context, the claim by the Ghanaian Ambassador to the Security Council that American mistakes and the delayed action of the munitions used (essentially anti-personnel mines) led to civilian deaths should be considered. It is illegal under Protocol II to the Geneva Conventions to use such weapons against civilians. Although mistakes often occur in a military operation, any such civilian casualties are to be deplored and should be avoided at all costs.

The alleged use of such weapons near centers of civilian population raises a question mark over the justification for the level of force used in the American raid. Such a random instrument of death smacks of the terrorism that the Americans themselves condemn. International law recognizes, however, that military operations do not always proceed smoothly and that collateral damage may occur as the result of an attack on a military target (although there is a duty to take precautions against such an event). The level of the American response has been justified by an American Naval Officer:

> ... we may fairly ask if alternative plans of military action would have reduced the risk of collateral damage. The United States could have used a commando-style raid to insert, destroy pre-selected targets, and extract. Though this might have been feasible, proportionality does not require a state to disregard the risks to its own forces. ... The United States made a conscious decision on a particular type of action. It also made a significant effort to conform with the requirement of proportionality consistent with what it viewed as reasonable risks to its forces. Its choice was reasonable, given the circumstances, and, although a close question, the result was within the standards of international law.

The American representative to the Security Council called his nation's action "necessary and proportionate" while the rhetoric of the Libyan Ambassador labeled it a "barbaric, savage air raid." Neither is an unbiased or objective source, although *prima facie* the American action seems to have been a reasonable and proportionate reaction.

This lack of objectivity, caused by the fundamentally political nature of the Security Council and of the United Nations in general, and the absence of an impartial adjudicator to impose a level of judicial rigor on the proceedings, is the crux of the problem in establishing the legality of the use of force in this incident.

Moving from proportionality to the question of complicity, this issue remains uncertain. In all of the debates or scholarly writings considered, we do not find a conclusive answer to our question: were the Libyan government accomplices in the placing of the bomb in the Berlin discotheque in April 1986? All we have is the word of the American government and its allies, admittedly biased sources. Against them, the protestations of the Libyans and those sympathetic to their plight (or at least opposed to the American government) none of which is considered by any judicial authority, with each side applying its own standards of proof to its actions.

After examining the facts leading up to the American air strike and the relevant international law, we can conclude that if the Libyan government was indeed part of the plot to bomb the "La Belle" night-club, and if it was planning further such attacks on American targets, then the American government was entitled to act. Such action was only justified if the only reasonable way for the United States to protect itself and its citizens was to bomb selected targets on Libyan soil. Such action must have been proportional to the ends desired and not intended as a reprisal or revenge attack.

Although the question of proportionality can only be conclusively answered by an independent military analysis, the American action seems to have fallen just inside the parameters of an acceptable response to an imminent terrorist attack, despite the mistakes made in the actual execution of the attack.

More difficult to determine is the issue of Libyan guilt. As the Americans will not give details of their evidence, it is impossible to properly answer this question. Without a legal (rather than political) forum with mandatory jurisdiction to consider and pronounce on this evidence, we cannot say if the American action was illegal or not.

Because of this lack of legal rigor and enforceability with regard to the use of force in international law, the prediction of Derek Bowett in 1972 has come to pass:

> Not surprisingly, as states have grown increasingly disillusioned about the capacity of the Security Council to afford them protection against what they would regard as illegal and highly injurious conduct directed against them, they have resorted to self-help in the form of reprisals and have acquired the confidence that, in so doing, they will not incur anything more than a formal censure from the Security Council. The law on reprisals is, because of its divorce from actual practice, rapidly degenerating to a stage where its normative character is in question.

Ignoring this problem will only continue to lead to tragedies in the Middle East and elsewhere. It is imperative that the states making up the United Nations acknowledge this problem and deal with it. It is evident from the massive mobilization of forces in the Gulf War that when there is political (or perhaps economic) will, the UN (and specifically the

Security Council) can enforce its resolutions. This will must be brought to bear more often, before the rogue states of the international system drag the world back to a system of anarchy.

Chapter 7

In Conclusion

There are several possibilities that support the facts and data available. The first possible reason for the raid is the Libyan interference and influence in Africa. As seen earlier, Qaddafi and Reagan each had their own opposing designs for Africa, with Reagan seeing Libya as a threat to American interests there. Libyan involvement in Nicaragua could be another reason.

President Reagan made it very clear to the American people that he considered Nicaragua to be a major threat to America.

Another possible reason could be the Libyan association with the Soviet Union, even though it may have been a result of American pressure. Reagan considered the Soviet Union to be a threat to the world and saw Libya as a way to put the Soviets in their place, and prove American dominance.

Still another possibility for the attack on Libya, rather than other terrorist countries like Syria or Iran, is that Libya was the weakest. Libya had the least Soviet support, the weakest military, was geographically the easiest for an attack, and Qaddafi was the most vocal.

The final and all encompassing possibility for the attack on Libya is that Ronald Reagan wanted to show the world that America was once again a dominant world figure. Show the world's nations that even the Soviet Union could not stand up to the United States, and that it was worthwhile to have America as a friend.

The facts seem to disprove the rhetoric from the Reagan Administration that the 1986 raid on Libya was a U.S. response toward a terrorist act. The only thing announced from the Administration just prior to and just after the raid was about Libya's involvement in terrorism and how the U.S. policy toward terrorism needed to be enforced. It has been shown that this enforcement in itself was inconsistent with other actions/policies of the Administration, or at least a highly selective enforcement.

This is not to say that the raid had nothing to do with trying to curb terrorism, because somewhere near the bottom of the list of objectives antiterrorism was probably there. It was shown that the Reagan Administration did not have an accepted or standard definition for terrorism, and an example of this confusion was demonstrated when Reagan denounced the 1983 attack on the marines in Beirut as an act of terrorism, even though he previously argued that terrorism was attacks against helpless civilians.

Reagan also cited his reason for the raid on Libya as following the U.S. policy of acting when proof of terrorism was found, but did not act when evidence was available linking countries such as Iran, Syria, North Korea, Soviet Union, Cuba, Lebanon, etc. It has become apparent that the word "terrorism" was one used when years of attempts to decapitate the Libyan regime, and even assassinate its leader, had failed.

There seems to be considerable data to support the alternate line of thought that the conflict with Libya, and eventually the raid, was about global dominance, the tough American image, Soviet containment, and U.S. interests in Africa and the Middle East. This different line of thought on the subject may lend to the possible conclusion that the Reagan Doctrine of containing communism and usurping unfriendly regimes was not about solving the problem of international terrorism or enforcing an American anti-terrorism policy.

After analyzing the Reagan Doctrine, foreign policy, and attitude toward Libya since 1981, it is highly plausible that the 1986 raid on Libya was not solely a response to international terrorism as the Reagan administration proclaimed, but a predetermined objective intended to decapitate the leadership of the Libyan regime.

About the Author

The author, a retired U.S. Army Officer, is currently a Supervisory Special Agent with a United States Federal Agency. He has a long-standing interest in history and politics, which he pursued through a Bachelor Degree in Political Science from the University of South Carolina at Aiken.

Other academic accomplishments include a Masters of Public Administration from the University of Oklahoma, and a Juris Doctor Degree from Oklahoma City University School of Law. The author is currently licensed to practice law, and is a member of the Oklahoma Bar, District of Columbia Bar, and the Federal Bar for the Western District of Oklahoma.

In addition to having over 23 years of government service and having written numerous papers on political and military subject matter, the author is a family man who enjoys several hobbies and "leisure time" accomplishments:

- Qualified parachutist
- Holds a First Degree Black Belt in Taekwondo
- Master Scuba Diver and Dive Master
- Has a Private Pilot Rating
- Enjoys a good game of chess

Bibliography/Sources

Primary Sources

Air War College Research Report, No. AU-AWC-88-043, Air University. "Libya Raid," Chapter V, Command and Control and Communications Lessons Learned by Colonel Stephen E. Anno and Lieutenant Colonel William E. Einspahr.

Congressional Quarterly Almanac, Vol XLII, 1986.

Public Papers Of The Presidents, Ronald Reagan. U.S. Government Printing Office, Vol I, 1986.

Public Report Of The Vice President's Task Force On Combating Terrorism. Feb 1986.

U.S. Department Of State Bulletin, Vol 86, Number 2111, June 1986.

U.S. Department Of State Bulletin, Vol 86, Number 2113, Aug 1986.

Internet Sources

Operation El Dorado Canyon.
http://members.lycos.co.uk/Hornet/index-19.html

Libya: The U.S. Air and Sea Attacks on Libya in 1986.
http://ourworld.compuserve.com/homepages/dr_ibrahim_ighneiwa/March86c.htm

Secondary Sources

Barber, James D. The Presidential Character. Prentice-Hall, 1992.

Bearman, Johnathan. Qaddafi's Libya. Zed Books LTD, New Jersey, 1986.

Billington, James H. "Realism And Vision In Foreign Policy." Foreign Affairs; America And The World 1986. Pergamon Press, New York, 1987.

Broyles, William. "The Real Strategy In The Libya Bombing," US News And World Report. May 12, 1986.

Crabb, Cecil; Holt, Pat. Invitation To Struggle: Congress, The President And Foreign Policy. CQ Press, Wash DC, 1984.

Davis, Brian L. Qaddafi, Terrorism And The Origins Of The U.S. Attack On Libya. Praeger, New York, 1990.

Dougherty, James; Pfaltzgraff, Robert. American Foreign Policy; FDR To Reagan. Harper & Row Publishers, New York, 1986.

Elwarfully, Mahmound G. Imagery And Ideology In U.S. Policy Toward Libya. University of Pittsburgh Press, 1988.

Emery, Noemie. "When It Takes." National Review, Feb.25, Vol. 54, Issue 3.

Geyelin, Philip. "The Reagan Crisis." Foreign Affairs; America And The World. Pergamon Press, New York, 1987.

Irewhitt, Henry. "A New War And New Risks." U.S. News And World Report, April 28, 1986.

Kaldor, Mary; Anderson, Paul. Mad Dogs, The U.S. Raid On Libya. Pluto Press Limited, 1986.

Kegley, Charles; Wittkopf, Eugene. American Foreign Policy, Pattern And Process. St Martin's Press, 1987.

Kidder, Rushworth. Violence And Terrorism. "Terrorism In The United States," Annual Editions, Dushkin Publishing Group, 1993.

Kidder, Rushworth. Violence And Terrorism. "Terrorism In The United States," Annual Editions, Dushkin Publishing Group, 1993.

Manning, Robert. "In Western Europe, Strains Among Friends." U.S. News And World Report, Apr 28, 1986.

Nathan, James; Oliver, James. Foreign Policy Making And The America Political System. Little, Brown and Company, Boston, 1987.

Oakley, Robert. Foreign Affairs; America And The World. "International Terrorism." Pergamon Press, New York, 1987.

Prunckun, Henry W; Mohr, Philip B. "Military Deterrence of International Terrorism: An Evaluation of Operation El Dorado Canyon." Studies In Conflict & Terrorism, Jul-Sep97, Vol. 20, Issue 3.

Sicker, Martin. The Making Of A Pariah State: The Adventurist Politics Of Muammar Qaddafi. Praeger Publications, New York, 1987.

Spanier, John; Uslaner, Eric. <u>American Foreign Policy Making And The Democratic Dilemmas</u>. Brooks/Cole Publishing Company, California, 1989.

St John, Bruce. <u>Qaddafi's World Design: Libyan Foreign Policy</u>. Saqi Books, 1987.

Swomley, John M. "The Ultimate Rogue Nation." <u>Humanist</u>, Jan/Feb 01, Vol. 61 Issue 1.

Whitaker, Mark; Walcot, John. <u>"Raid On Libya, A New Kind Of War."</u> <u>Newsweek</u>, Apr 28, 1986.

Whitaker, Mark. "Targeting A 'Mad Dog.'" <u>Newsweek</u>, Apr 21, 1986.

Index